A Gypsy and a Rebel:
Lillian Urmston in the Spanish Civil War

Linda Palfreeman
and
Alicia García López

The Clapton Press

The Clapton Press Limited
38 Thistlewaite Road
London E5 0QQ

www.theclaptonpress.com

ISBN 978-1-913693-37-4

This publication is part of the project "Transnational humanitarian medical action and technological innovation in spaces of confinement (1870-1950)." Grant (PID2019-104581GB-I00), funded by MCIN/AEI/10.13039/501100011033.

Table of Contents

Foreword

When the Public and Commercial Services Union (PCS) moved to new offices in Liverpool, they named their new meeting rooms after socialists who had strong links to the North-West region. One room was designated 'Robert Tressel', after the author of *The Ragged Trousered Philanthropist* and another, 'Lillian Urmston', in homage to those who travelled to support the Republicans in the Spanish Civil War.

This is how I first learnt about Lillian and the role she played in the fight against fascism in Spain. I knew about the brave men who left their families to join the International Brigades, so I was fascinated to find out about an ordinary working-class young woman who went from the small town of Stalybridge, in Northwest England, to the frontline in war-torn Spain. Lillian's social conscience and political convictions took her a long way from home. She could only have imagined what awaited her in Spain, yet she knew she could not stand by and do nothing.

Lillian worked in several emergency medical facilities on the frontline, where she saw and experienced all the horrors of war and helped save many lives. However, as a nurse and a woman she remained one of the many forgotten heroes. Lillian Urmston was a truly courageous and inspirational woman whose fight against fascism and injustice deserves to be recognised. I am so grateful that my union has created a lasting tribute to her, that is seen by everyone who visits our offices, and that her story is finally being told.

Laura Knotts, Industrial Officer for PCS Union
Unite North West
Jack Jones House
Liverpool

1.   Lillian in nurse's uniform (location unknown) c. 1937.

Preface

Lillian Urmston was just nineteen years old when she offered her services as a nurse in the Spanish Civil War. Though imbued with a strong sense of social justice, she had no political affiliations. Her reasons for going to Spain, she affirmed, were purely humanitarian; she volunteered because she was convinced that it was 'the right thing to do': she saw a people in need and was compelled to go to their aid.

It was precisely this lack of political bias, however, that would cause Lillian problems, even before she got to Spain. It would take her several attempts to convince those of the Communist controlled Spanish Medical Aid Committee (SMAC) that she was the perfect candidate for the role of wartime nurse. This sense of suspicion was something that Lillian felt throughout her time in Spain and while she was praised by all with whom she worked—from the nursing assistants she trained to the surgeons she herself assisted, she felt she was treated as something of an outsider by her nursing peers, many of whom were members of the Communist Party before going to Spain, or became members during the war.

Nevertheless, 'Our Lillian', as she became affectionately known in her hometown of Stalybridge, stayed true to her convictions. Her actions were governed by her sense of empathy and social justice, and she would not be told what to think by others. This included the political commissars and Communist spies by whom she would be labelled 'too conceited to learn'. Too conceited to learn, or too strong in her moral convictions to succumb to Communist propaganda—it is left to the reader to decide.

When an emergency arose during a time of rest, and in the absence of superiors from whom to seek guidance, Lillian and nursing colleague, Dorothy Low, responded to a request for help from an équipe of Americans. They had been ordered to create a frontline hospital and were in urgent need of nurses. Lillian and Dorothy sacrificed their well-earned break to render their vital assistance. For this, they were vilified by the rest of the group, and on their return, nobody would speak to them, until, that is, the arrival of Len Crome, Chief Medical Officer of the 35th Army Corps, to which Lillian was now attached.[1] Crome diffused the situation with the tact and diplomacy for which he was renowned, and peaceful relations were restored within the group. However, it is little wonder that, as the war progressed, determined to continue to do all she could for the Spanish people, Lillian would work with Spanish medical équipes whenever the opportunity arose. This itself would be used against her by Communist spy, Winifred Bates, self-styled political commissar for the nursing contingent.

Lillian's experience in Spain proved of vital interest to the civil and military authorities in Britain, during preparations for the coming Second World War. She would go on to serve as a nurse with the British Army, in various overseas posts, before being seriously wounded. She returned to Spain several times, to the areas where she had worked as a nurse, to visit the people whose 'guts and courage' she would never forget, and who welcomed her with open arms.

Introduction

A failed military coup in Spain, in July 1936, led to three years of bloody civil war in which an estimated half a million people died.[1] The insurgent forces, led by General Francisco Franco, received significant financial and military backing from Nazi Germany and fascist Italy, whilst the Republic relied chiefly on aid from the Soviet Union. Britain joined other countries including France and the United States, in adopting a policy of 'non-intervention', arguably designed to stop the hostilities from escalating internationally. Despite this policy (indeed, largely as a response to it) Socialist and Communist organisations in these countries actively supported the republican government and sponsored volunteer participation. Some 2,500 British men joined in the armed fight in defence of Spanish democracy, together with over 33,000 other volunteers from 53 different nations of the world, as part of the fighting force that became known as the International Brigades.[2]

Many thousands more became involved in providing humanitarian aid. Britons were no exception. Anti-fascist movements, peace organisations, political and religious groups all came out in support of the Spanish Government. Since the seminal study of Jim Fyrth (1986) there has been a steadily growing historiography on British involvement in this relief work.[3] The works of Tom Buchanan (1977, 2017) deal with various aspects of the impact of the Spanish Civil War on Britain,[4] while Lewis Mates (2008) provides a sense of how local and regional concerns in England influenced specific individual and collective left-wing responses.[5] More recently, however, Mason (2017) points out that much of the historiography to date has focused on left-wing politics with far less attention given to the humanitarian enterprises themselves.[6] This approach neglects essential components of humanitarian action, namely, the individuals who provided assistance in time of crisis as well as particulars of the emergency care implemented and the many and varied challenges they encountered along the way. The present book seeks to help redress this imbalance.

The focus here is on the medical contribution made by volunteer nurse, Lillian Urmston. In telling Lillian's story we also seek to give increased visibility to the roles played by female humanitarian volunteers (chiefly, nurses) in the Spanish Civil War—individuals who have been historically underrepresented in this field until relatively recently and whose roles have, to some extent, been misunderstood. The reasons British women gave for engaging with Spain were diverse, often inconsistent, and even contradictory. They were women seeking to access the male dominated public arena and to do so they had to free themselves (consciously or otherwise) from the bonds of traditional femininity. Women involved in medical and other humanitarian relief have been frequently represented in histories of the Spanish Civil War (and in war histories in general) as 'loving angels or compassionate mothers who took care of victims as if they were their own children'.[7] Lillian Urmston, as we shall see, was destined to be a rebel. Her story helps to deconstruct this stereotypical view.

Nurses rarely wrote official reports or published technical manuals during or after the war, as did their male colleagues.[8] Instead, in order to understand women's experiences including, crucially, the development of medical knowledge and expertise, and the implementation of care, we must turn to a wide range of ego-documents such as 'letters, diaries, memoirs, autobiographies, oral histories, and also such personally composed items as scrapbooks, [and] photograph albums'.[9] Often judged as lacking in scientific value, such documents have frequently been overlooked in the history of both humanitarianism and medicine. We will demonstrate that, on the contrary, women's expertise, in this case, that of nurse Lillian Urmston, is essential in gaining a fuller understanding of the development and practice of frontline medical care during the Spanish Civil War. While Lillian did not leave a memoir or diary, she did compile a scrapbook of news cuttings and photographs[10]—mementos of her time in Spain, and once back in Britain, amidst preparations for the coming Second World War, she published a series of articles in the *Nursing Mirror*, based on her experience as a nurse in the Medical Service of the International Brigades.[11] Some years later, she was interviewed by authors Dave Corkill and Stuart Rawnsley for their book *The Road to Spain*.[12] The interview is preserved in the archive of the Tameside Local Studies Centre in Ashton-under-Lyne.[13] These various fragments might not attract the acclaim attained by the neat publications of Douglas Jolly or Josep Trueta on wartime surgery, or Gerald Shirlaw's manuals on civil defence, but together they form a valuable legacy, documenting the day-to-day work of a frontline nurse in wartime, in all its often tragic, untidy reality—the 'make-do-and mend' of it when materials and medicines were in short supply: the ingenuity and inventiveness involved in feeding patients and creating hospitals in the midst of farmyard filth.

Urmston was part of the British medical community that went to the aid of the Republic after the outbreak of war in Spain. Hers was, she insisted, an undertaking motivated by humanitarian rather than political instincts. The largest and most renowned medical unit to leave Britain for Spain was that of the Spanish Medical Aid to Spain Committee (SMAC) and its wartime work has been documented in previous studies.[14] As soon as she learned of its existence, Lillian Urmston would bombard the Committee with letters until she was finally accepted as a volunteer for Spain.

Lillian's recollections do not present a chronologically accurate account of the war and its events, nor does she attempt to furnish us with details of a political or military nature. Instead, she gives us a first-hand glimpse into the pioneering medical work carried out in Spain that would revolutionise military medical care and would prove of vital importance to the civilian and military medical services in Britain, both before and during the Second World War.

Chapter One:
Lillian's early years in Stalybridge

'Our Lillian' made her entrance into the world in Stalybridge, Manchester, on 7 June 1915. Born in wartime Britain, she lived in less than affluent circumstances in Copely Street, with her parents, her two sisters, Mary and Hannah, and younger brother, Harry. A robust and independent child, one of Lillian's earliest and abiding memories was her pride in her colourful ancestry. Much to the chagrin of her mother, this was something openly encouraged by her father:

> I'm told my first two teeth were cut on a Victoria Cross that had been won by a Canadian soldier. Mother insisted that was lucky and I'd have a good career. Father wasn't interested. He was more anxious to instill into me that I was a descendant of Jack Cade, the rebel. My mother hated this idea that Jack Cade was always instilled into my mind and the more mother disliked it, the more I wallowed in the story.[1]

Proof of the family's lineage was to be found in documents jealously guarded by an aunt of Lillian's father. It was her father's dearest wish that Lillian would one day inherit the documents, but they were somehow lost, or disappeared, during the time that she was training as a nurse. 'Mother wasn't too keen on the idea of Jack Cade having been a rebel,' she recalls, 'but the more I've read about him since, the more proud I am that, in a small way, perhaps I tried to carry on his tradition.'[2]

Lillian was also proud of the fact that she had gypsy ancestors. She remembers that gypsies were always welcome at their home and that, as a child, she often used to wander off with them and would be brought safely home just as her parents were beginning to worry. Though fiercely independent, she admits having been 'terribly close' to her father who encouraged her to think for herself from the earliest age and to act according to her conscience. It was also her father who fostered her love of nature and the outdoors and, above all, her love of books. 'No political books,' Lillian was keen to point out, 'Father didn't trust politics.'

Lillian's father, something of a dreamer, had hoped to earn his living as a horse trainer and in his youth was employed at Lord Lonsdale's stables on the outskirts of Penrith in Cumbria's Eden Valley. It was here that he met the young woman with whom he would fall in love and who would become the mother of his children. Any romantic notions conjured by the tale are quashed by Lillian's somewhat dispassionate, and typically pragmatic, account of events. As a young man, explains Lillian, her father had wanted to become a horse trainer. 'However, he met my mother. Mother wanted a settled life. She didn't want a skinny jockey-type husband, so dad moved into the steel business.' Marriage compelled the young Urmston to put aside his boyhood dreams and join Taylor, Lang and Co., a textile machinery manufacturer based in Stalybridge. The company was just one of the firms to be very badly hit during the Depression years (1929–1930s). The management did its best to share the work fairly among the workforce, devising a rota by which each employee worked reduced hours. This, believed Lillian, was a sensible and humane response to an otherwise dreadful situation.[3]

Lillian attended St Paul's Elementary School and the local Primary School where she recalls having been 'very fortunate in teachers'. She remembers her first teacher, Miss Hettie Hassle, 'of unknown parentage', 'adopted by a spinster lady who gave her a teacher training education'. Lillian recalls Miss Hassle's love for the outdoors, books (particularly poetry) and reading. She inspired Lillian's own love of reading by constantly lending her books. She was further encouraged to read by her headmaster, Mr Jones, 'an intellectual Welsh man with (I am now convinced) socialist tendencies. I am absolutely sure of that now, affirms Lillian. 'They wanted to develop children's brains and they helped me with schoolbooks when they thought we couldn't afford them'.

At the age of 12, she went on to the local Secondary School. While not keen on Mathematics or Algebra, she developed her keen interest in history. She also had a flair for language, and edited the school magazine, as her sister had done before her. It was here that Lillian's organisational skills and her qualities of leadership also began to emerge. 'I suppose I was always the leader if anything had to be done. I was always chosen. I suppose I led people by the nose,' she admits, 'I certainly organised all the theatricals at school and things like that and I loved music, and I was always allowed to choose the songs to sing at the annual concert, and so on.'

When school leaving time came, however, Lillian discovered that there were very few options open to girls, especially those from families of scarce economic means. She was sensitive to her father's distress at being unable to fund her further education, or even to allow her to take up the scholarships she was awarded. He would point out that there were other families much worse off than theirs—people who had lost their menfolk in the First World War and mothers who were caring for a family on a pittance of allowance. Lillian took this very much in her stride and determined to do what she could 'to boost the family coffers'. Nevertheless, she did have her own standards with regard to the chosen profession and refused to be bound entirely by the restraints of gender:

> You could win scholarships, which I did, but we never had any money to take them up. So, when it came for time for deciding, some teachers wanted to pay for an apprenticeship to a hairdresser and I thought that was damn silly. My eldest sister was, but I just couldn't do anything like that. I loved the outdoors and I heard of this position going in the market with the florist, and I thought

how wonderful it would be to be with flowers.[4]

She enjoyed the job for which she soon found she had a flair and was very much appreciated by those with whom she worked. The florists, the 'flighty and modern' Wilcox sisters of Duckinfield had boyfriends and drove around in sports cars which was definitely not approved of, recalls Lillian, 'but they quickly taught me how to break reeds and arrange bouquets, and they found I had the knack of sympathy for dealing with people.' She earned 30 shillings per week, which she saw, at the time, as 'an enormous sum for a teenage girl'. Nevertheless, at the end of the week she would always find more money had been put into her bag, along with a generous supply of flowers, while a neighbouring stallholder loaded her up with vegetables.

Lillian's parents were ardent churchgoers of Protestant persuasion. They subscribed to the Christian belief in 'doing good' and instilled this in their children. It was something that Lillian felt quite deeply. She taught in Sunday School and was in the Girl Guide movement. She recalls an early event that impressed upon her the importance of social compassion. It was on her twice-weekly trips into Stalybridge to do the 'big shop'.

I will never forget that if it was the half-term holiday and I went during the day, the feeling that I had to cross the road when I was passing the local Labour Exchange because of the queues of men, some of whom I knew by sight, and young lads, teenagers, they were standing there looking hungry, depressed and ashamed, and I used to feel ashamed that I'd even glanced at them because I felt it was adding to their misery. And then I heard stories of the way they were treated, when the money was pushed across the counter it was often pushed so that coins fell onto the floor, when the man had to touch his cap and pick them up they were told: 'Hurry up, hurry up, there's a long queue behind you, you know, get out of the way.'

In retrospect Lillian realised that what she was experiencing was a certain social and political awakening. 'These were political inklings beginning in me,' she explains, 'but I didn't recognise them as such in those days.' Until then, Lillian had been largely unaware of what she later recognized as the 'terrific class structure' existing in her hometown of Stalybridge. She remembers being conscious of the fact that on Sunday mornings, all the local gentry went to church wearing clean white gloves and Lillian's family did not. She imagined them later enjoying sedate pursuits in the privacy of their own homes. However, this class difference did nothing to sour the relationship between families—on the contrary, as Lillian explains: 'there were various aldermen, all Conservative, I remember that,' she adds, 'and yet, without exception they were all my friends, and I will never forget the number of books they lent me.'

Thanks to the generosity of such friends, Lillian became an avid reader of poetry—from the classics like Wordsworth and Swinburne to the more modern poets such as Yorkshireman, Samuel Laycock. It was her father, explains Lillian, who taught her to appreciate the works of Laycock, 'the poet who wrote about Stalybridge sacrificing herself for the American Civil War—how Stalybridge, a thriving cotton town, went bankrupt so that the Civil War should be won by the right side in America.'

Lillian left her position with the florist after being attracted by an advertisement in the local paper for a vacant post at the local artificial silk factory. The girl appointed would learn the trade by training and working in the mill and then go on to become assistant to two brothers, World War veterans, George and Harry Byron. The brothers' aim was to create much needed employment for the local area. Lillian got the job and for a time was very happy at the mill. Her employers treated her kindly and soon began to show great trust in her abilities. They gave her all the support they could and encouraged her visits to the Manchester Stock Exchange, a learning experience that she particularly enjoyed. However, Lillian eventually found that she could not bear the noise of working at the factory. 'I don't know whether it was the gypsy blood in me or Jack Cade coming out,' she explained later, 'but I was stifled and so desperately unhappy with the result that I threw myself more and more into the Girl Guide and Brownie movements and the Cubs as well.'

The underlying cause of Lillian's unrest was that she had always wanted to become a doctor, but she knew the family's poor economic situation meant that it would be impossible for her to study Medicine. When she turned seventeen, Lillian decided to broach the topic of her future with her father. She had come to the conclusion that the most accessible alternative would be a career in nursing. So, encouraged by her father, she set about applying for positions as a trainee nurse. However, in the early stages, things went far from smoothly. 'I wrote to Queen Mary's in Carshalton, Surrey,' recalls Lillian, 'and mother tore up the papers. No daughter of hers was going to move away from home. It just wasn't done. You stayed at home and your mother looked after you and helped to choose a husband for you, I suppose.' There were boys among Lillian's friends, at the time, but not a particular boyfriend because, she explains, 'I always vaguely seemed to know that I would have a career of some kind,' and she did not want boyfriends interfering with her plans.

Eventually, a compromise was reached, and Lillian was taken on at the local Lake Hospital in Ashton-under-Lyne. The minimum age requirement was eighteen-and-a-half, and she persuaded one of her more rebellious (paternal) uncles, 'a terrific character', to testify that she was that age. She began training within a week, reporting for duty at 11.00 am on a Sunday morning, carrying a medical dictionary that she had bought second hand 'and that I was very proud of and understood nothing in it at all'.

She remembers her first matron, Miss Millie Whitten, as very progressive but a strict disciplinarian. Many of her cotrainees were Irish girls whose uppermost objective was to gain stable employment and Lillian observed that their vocation was, at times, as questionable as their credentials.

> When they came from Ireland, nobody really seemed to bother about what grade they had reached at school or what their hobbies had been or anything like that. When I asked about this, they looked in horror and said, 'God, Lillian! We're Catholics!' as though that explained everything. I was always puzzled about that but I quickly learned that the Irish knew how to look after themselves. They stayed in bed late as they were allowed to go to early morning mass and at least three-quarters of them didn't but they stayed in bed anyway. So, we always had a certain degree of loathing for them. Yet, later on in the Spanish Civil War they were the nurses who used to collect money from patients and send it to Spanish Medical Aid.

While she was training during the early 1930s, Lillian occasionally stayed with Welsh relatives. Here, again to her delight, the name Jack Cade would come up in conversation, 'but it was always in whispers,' she adds, 'because in Wales, in those days, you didn't talk too much about rebels. People were getting very Tory minded, especially when they'd had a Labour Government for a short period.'

Lillian progressed steadily through training, eventually becoming a State Registered Nurse and going on to study midwifery. It was at a stage, she recalls, when all the rules and regulations changed, and midwives, students included, had to do an enormous amount of paperwork—so much so, recalls Lillian that the nurses complained that they had more and more patients to look after and not enough time to look after the newborn babies. Lillian took this as an opportunity to gain experience. They were so busy rushing into the office to fill in forms as well as carry out their nursing duties, she explains, that when trainee nurses were out on district calls, they would be happy for Lillian to accompany them on her days off.

From Ashton-under-Lyne Lillian moved to Manchester where she described the dreadful conditions in which women were having babies, 'one after another', in slum areas of Stalybridge. These were, for the most part, noted Lillian, staunchly Catholic areas. Even though Lillian had only been the one to hold their hand and help with the baby, the women were very grateful. Many of them lived in dire conditions with little or no assistance. The father dared not stay home from work to help because it would mean a reduction in his desperately needed wage; worse still, he might lose his job. The other children of the household were simply sent out into the street or onto the tenement steps to wait. All this had a 'terrific effect' on Lillian. 'There again, I suppose my political leanings—'awakenings'—were being aroused,' she reflects.

By 1934, Lillian had become firm friends with a nurse who was going to become a missionary. She was going to Abyssinia to marry her fiancé and she tried to persuade Lillian to go with her. Meanwhile, Lillian also formed a close friendship with Quaker, Ursula Summerville. Ursula introduced Lillian to her brother who ran a mission hospital in India. Though she furnishes us with no details, it must be assumed that Lillian enjoyed a more than friendly relationship with young Summerville, as she later affirms: 'He took it for granted that I would go out and join him once I'd got my diplomas and degrees and so on.' Any budding plans must surely have been affected by the turn of events that was to follow.

The friend preparing to join her fiancé in Abyssinia allowed Lillian to read their assiduous correspondence, presumably to help persuade her to go with them. Then, suddenly, the letters stopped. Some days later, the young nurse received word from one of the senior chaplains in the mission explaining that the Italian forces had reached the base in Addis Ababa where her fiancé was stationed. He had just recently qualified as a doctor and was out doing medical work when he was captured. After days of anguish and uncertainty, the young woman received a phone call while she was working on the ward opposite Lillian's. Lillian takes up the story:

> I heard a noise like an animal in labour and as I had a quiet spell I rushed down to see if she had a difficult patient, probably someone dying, and she was sobbing her heart out in the kitchen and she'd got her head wrapped in a roller towel trying to control the noise. She had just heard about her fiancé who had been tortured and killed for treating gassed captives.

Utterly distraught, she confided in Lillian that she no longer had any idea what her future might be. 'I don't know what I'm going to do now,' she cried, 'because all my life was wrapped up in him and his work.' This was a harsh reminder to Lillian, if ever she had needed one, that she must make her own way in life, independent of any possible pressure and persuasion from others—including potential marriage partners.[5]

When Lillian and her colleagues had a few minutes' break on night duty, they used to read the newspapers. There was a wide selection available to them as private patients were usually brought the *Guardian* or the *News Chronicle* while others read the *Daily Herald* or the *Daily Mail*. Lillian read them all and was extremely well informed on the affairs of the day. It was a time when Europe was becoming increasingly threatened by the rise of fascist regimes. By the mid-1930s, autocratic regimes had been imposed on most central, eastern and southern European countries. One of the few exceptions was Spain where elections in 1931 led to the proclamation of the Second Republic. However, the road to democracy would be far from easy and subsequent years would be marked by social and political division in the country.

Lillian knew that war in Europe was inevitable, and she explained the situation to her fellow nurses. 'Look, there's going to be a war,' she announced, 'and we are going to need our training. And it's going to be a terrible war because the more I read about it, it's going to be total.' From that moment onwards, Lillian decided that she would equip herself with the knowledge and skills that she thought would be most useful in wartime. She announced to colleagues that she was going to study tropical diseases under Sir Patrick Manson, the world specialist and founder of the London School of Hygiene and Tropical Medicine. Treating tropical diseases requires a special kind of nursing and Lillian knew that she was up to the job. 'Tropical fevers leave you weak and depressed and demoralised', she explained, 'and you've got to give the right kind of sympathy without too much sugar attached.' This gives us further insight into Lillian's character. She was empathetic and compassionate, but not to the point of indulgence. She was firmly convinced that practical solutions had to be found to the most terrible of problems.

Lillian and a colleague travelled to the London hospital where Manson was working. They were given a tour of the wards and were invited to work there for a short period to confirm whether they had the skills (and inclination) necessary for looking after people with the debilitating diseases in question. For Lillian, there was never any question: 'always deep down with me there was the thought that it was going to be part of my life and I absolutely thrived on it'. Furthermore, probably recognizing Lillian's interest and aptitude, Manson made a fuss of her, which spurred her on even more strongly to do well. Meanwhile, she had taken her state final nursing exams and was awaiting the results, though she admitted to being quietly confident: 'I had a feeling I'd passed. I knew I had somehow.'

At this time, the hospital was visited by a nurse from the Queen Alexandra's Imperial Military Nursing Service (QUAIMNS). Lillian recalls that she was in civilian clothes, and she was talking about the glory of serving one's country. Again, Lillian was more interested in the practical matters such as the duties involved. She made known her opinion that nurses in the First World War had not been well enough organised and that there had been a great deal of waste at the base hospitals. The nurse assured her that there would be plenty of improvements made in the coming war and that Territorials were urgently needed, especially newly trained nurses, and more especially ones who had obtained degrees other than midwifery. So, together with a colleague, Lillian joined the Territorial Army Nursing Service. Shortly afterwards, she answered a press advert for a Staff Nurse in the Lake District. Her father had always wanted her to go there to see the place near Penrith where he had been 'wonderfully happy' and he knew that she would love the open countryside. She was offered the position and would go on to spend six months there. It was while Lillian was in the Lake District that civil war broke out in Spain.

Chapter Two:
The Spanish Civil War

Spain was a country suffering from a prolonged period of political unrest. Millions of people lived in abject poverty, while some enormously wealthy individuals owned vast agricultural estates. Over half the population was illiterate and many children received no schooling at all, education being the preserve of the Catholic Church. The newly elected Republican government championed democracy, progress, and universal suffrage. It recognized that it was only through education that citizens could become emancipated. Free universal, secular education was established, and ambitious plans were drawn up to create thousands of new schools. Education would be compulsory and open to both girls and boys.

Sweeping social reforms were introduced, making clear the government's intentions to break up the extensive holdings of prominent landowners, and to diminish the powerful reactionary influence of the Church that lent its power and influence to maintaining the status quo. For privileged society, including some of the most powerful army generals, the promised social reforms represented a threat to what had been a hitherto advantaged existence, and they used all the means available to block them. Furthermore, from the moment the government was elected, monarchists and army officers began plotting its downfall.

When, in 1933, the Socialists broke their alliance with the liberal Republicans, it paved the way for a right-wing victory in the November elections. There followed the immediate revocation of the previous reforms. Employers cut wages and raised rents, evicting tenants and dismissing workers as they saw fit, while attempts at protests or strikes were met with merciless reprisals. On 6 October 1934, the Socialists called a general strike. Martial law was declared, and the strike failed in most of Spain. In the mining area of Asturias, however, socialists, anarchists, and communists united. They held out for almost three weeks under heavy bombardment and artillery fire from the Spanish Foreign Legion and Moorish troops under the command of General Francisco Franco. Some 2,000 miners were killed and over 30,000 political prisoners were taken. In the wake of this savage repression, the Republican-Socialist coalition was reformed into the Popular Front. It gained a narrow victory in the elections in February of 1936 and immediately began to revive earlier programmes of social reform.[1]

The right used agents provocateurs to incite social unrest and also orchestrated incidents of public disorder and violence as part of its plan to justify a military uprising. The subsequent imposition of an authoritarian regime would then be promoted as the only means of restoring law and order. General Emilio Mola headed the military rebellion which was finally launched on 18 July 1936. Though successful in the provincial capitals of conservative Castile, the insurgents failed to take control of the whole country. After an initial period of nationwide disorder and confusion and ferocious local fighting, Spanish territory became divided into 'Nationalist' zones (areas controlled by the rebels) and 'Loyalist' or Republican zones. This was the beginning of a long and bloody civil war.

Out of fascist solidarity (as well as for reasons of national interest) Hitler and Mussolini backed the rebels, supplying them with crucial military aid in the form of troops and weaponry. In return for Spanish gold, the Republic received aid on a much lesser scale from the Soviet Union, largely in the form of antiquated weaponry. The failure of the Republic to secure further armament was the direct result of the Treaty of Non-Intervention. With the supposed objective of confining the struggle within Spain, the Treaty prohibited all international military aid to either of the two sides in the conflict. It was signed by 27 countries including Italy, Germany, the Soviet Union and Great Britain. However, Nazi Germany and fascist Italy (and, on a lesser scale, Portugal) blatantly continued to supply the rebel forces with massive amounts of arms and troops. Consequently, the British Government's continued adherence to the policy of non-intervention was, to many citizens, completely unacceptable and, as if in a spirit of reparation, the British public launched nationwide demonstrations of support for the Spanish Republic.

British response to outbreak of war in Spain

More than 2,500 British volunteers took up arms in defence of the Republic, as part of the fighting force that came to be known as the International Brigades.[2] Many of them belonged to the Communist Party and many were intellectuals, but a wide range of professions and social classes were represented—above all, the working-class. Thousands of others organised meetings, concerts, fairs, and all manner of other events to raise funds to send humanitarian aid to Spain and to encourage support for the anti-fascist cause. The unions (including the Unemployed Workers' Union) played an important role in fundraising and factory workers also donated hours of their labour to build ambulances and repair lorries destined for Spain. Anti-fascist movements, peace organisations, political and religious groups all came out in support of the Spanish Government. One such association was the Relief Committee for Victims of Fascism headed by Isabel Brown. The Society of Friends and the Save the Children Fund also sent aid, particularly milk and other primary necessities for young children and infants.

Throughout Britain, more than 1,000 aid committees were especially created and millions of individuals, from every class and social circumstance donated food, clothing, medicines, and other essential provisions. Fleets of ships and lorries took these emergency rations to Spain and helped evacuate Spanish refugees. Other volunteers went out to Spain to establish and run hospitals, refuges, soup kitchens and schools.[3] Buchanan sums up the reaction of the British people:

> Fascism, in its many forms, appeared to offer a terrifying threat to democracy and to civilization itself. Thus, the outbreak of the Spanish Civil War in July 1936 was seized upon by many as the first occasion where fascism had been resisted by a people in arms, and provided a lesson in how this thuggish, nationalistic, and dictatorial force could be stopped. Moreover, they believed that, if Franco and his Fascist backers could be defeated in Spain, then countries such as Britain could be spared a similar ordeal.[4]

When war broke out the Republic could not meet the demand for medical attention and the government made a worldwide plea for help. There were two immediate reactions in Great Britain. The National Council of Labour (which united the Labour Party and the Trades Union Congress) launched a campaign to collect funds for the Republic. The other equally important reaction was the creation of the Spanish Medical Aid Committee (SMAC), the British committee largely responsible for sending medical teams to Spain, as well as vehicles, surgical equipment, and other medical matériel.

Spanish Medical Aid Committee

The SMAC was formed under the auspices of Dr Hyacinth Morgan, medical adviser to the TUC. Morgan sought the help of Communist Isabel Brown,[5] who had a great deal of experience in running committees of this kind, and the socialist, Dr Charles Brook. Brook called several well-known, left-wing, public figures to attend an initial meeting in a room of the Trade Union Club at 24, New Oxford Street, where he spoke about the need for medical help in Spain. A fundraising committee was created to purchase medical supplies and to send them to the Spanish Republic along with medical personnel. The Spanish Medical Aid Committee, or at least the main subcommittee which took executive action, was Communist controlled, though this was never openly admitted.[6] In order to maximise its appeal, the SMAC was always promoted as a non-political association with solely humanitarian intentions.[7] It enjoyed the cooperation of the Spanish Embassy, and the British government issued the permits needed to be able to buy and export the necessary medicines.

Communists, socialists, liberals and unionists all donated money to the SMAC. The National Council of Labour gave £1,000 to buy trucks and a car. The Society of Lithographic Artists, Designers, Engravers and Process Workers donated an *autochir* (or mobile operating theatre) for the medical unit sent out to Spain. As well as a team of medical personnel, the unit also comprised ambulances and other vehicles carrying a portable X-ray machine, electric generator, beds and other donated equipment.

Though the British Medical Association (BMA) refused to give the SMAC official backing, the general public's reaction to the committee was extremely generous, and there was also a tremendous response to the request for volunteers for service in Spain. Advertisements were placed in the national press asking for volunteer doctors, students, nurses, and other assistants prepared to work in Spain. They provoked an avalanche of replies, including one from Lillian Urmston. When she saw the appeal for medical volunteers in the *News Chronicle*, she wrote immediately to the SMAC, offering her services as a nurse. However, she would have to wait some considerable time for a reply.

Lillian was at pains to point out (then, as well as after the war) that politics had nothing to do with her decision. Nor was she aware of other nurses who had Communist or any other political tendencies before going to Spain. In fact, she explains, politics was almost a taboo topic in the hospital. 'If anyone in the Common Room were to say, "Oh, I wonder who will get in on the local council on voting day," there was an immediate outburst of: "No politics here!" It was the same if a patient mentioned politics on the wards.'[8]

Nevertheless, though she professed no political affiliation, Lillian most certainly had a strong political awareness, just as she was aware, from an early age, of the constraints of gender that would shape her destiny. It will be remembered, for example, that she thought the career options open to girls to be 'damn silly', and while her future life and work cannot be interpreted as a conscious attempt to free herself from the dominant nineteenth century gender ideology, she was determined that neither boyfriends nor husbands were going to hamper her opportunity of making a career for herself—even if it was in the recognizably female, 'nurturing' field of nursing.

Lillian knew that she had what it takes to nurse on a war front. (She could give 'the right kind of sympathy without too much sugar attached'.) Other women volunteers in Spain echoed Lillian Urmston's dismissal of what were considered traditionally feminine characteristics.[9] For example, Nan Green, who played a vital role as hospital administrator in Spain, refuted 'the ridiculous idea that I was going to Spain "to join my husband".'[10] Lillian found Nan friendly and supportive, unlike some of the other communist members of the group by whom she felt she was treated like an 'outsider'.[11]

It was clear to Lillian, from all she had read, that the Spanish Republic was the just cause to follow. The rebels were very well backed in both financial and military terms, while the Spanish Government was obviously short of everything and needed nurses. Her natural inclination was to go to the aid of the underdog. She was reminded of her early days as a trainee nurse, at the age of eighteen, when the ward was 'chock-full' of wounded veterans of the First World War.

Some of them were coughing their guts and their lungs out due to having been gassed. There was no cure in those days. You either died of bronchiolitis or cancer due primarily to the gas—mustard gas—that was used. And [...] on this ward they used to talk to me about their experiences and I used to be filled with horror that not enough had been done for them either during the war, or when they were wounded, and certainly not after the war. They considered themselves lucky to be alive, especially if they had a comfortable bed in a hospital. That's all they needed.[12]

Lillian found herself on night duty on Armistice Night. There was an atmosphere in the ward that night of 'the old war horse' she recalls. Memories both bitter and sweet were shared, and the place was filled with an incredible comradeship. Lillian felt she had to do something to mark the occasion.

That night the Superintendent had been round and she looked awfully tired and I knew she would have a good sleep so I whizzed round my friends and asked if they could nick a few eggs and I made scrambled eggs on toast and pots of tea and we carried it round the wards. And I just felt that night that there was something stirring in me that I was part of something that meant a great deal to the country and the individuals concerned.[13]

Lillian confided in her father about her desire to go and nurse in the Spanish war. He knew that she would do well at whatever task with which she was faced, but he felt compelled to offer practical advice. He was afraid she would end up like him, without much to show for a lifetime of work, and he tried to impress upon her the importance of earning money. Nevertheless, he also knew that in making the final decision about Spain, Lillian would follow her heart. He was not mistaken—she had already made up her mind but sought her father's blessing. She was bitterly disappointed, therefore, when she received no reply from the SMAC, and proceeded to bombard them with further letters of application. In the interim, while working at the Lake District nursing home she visited as much as she could of the area where her father had worked and where one or two people still remembered him as a stable lad.

Meanwhile, the first SMAC unit got ready to depart for Spain. It consisted of people from widely differing social backgrounds, medical experience, and political perspective. There were four qualified doctors and four student doctors accompanied by four nurses and two Australian women who would carry out secretarial and administrative duties. Six drivers, a photographer and two quartermasters completed the team that left New Oxford Street on 23 August 1936, in a convoy of Daimlers lent by the London Cooperative Funeral Department. The group, bound for Barcelona, was waved off from Victoria Station by some 10,000 people, including several London mayors, trade unionists and Arthur Greenwood, the leader of the Parliamentary Labour Party. It was the first British medical unit destined for Spain and, indeed, the first medical unit from any country to answer the call for help from the Republic. As such, the unit had immense political significance for the Spanish Republic, and crossing the frontier into Spain it was given a tumultuous reception.[14]

Still without word from the SMAC, Lillian sent a telegram demanding to know why they had not replied. She was answered by committee secretary, George Jeger, who invited her to London for an interview. She had some leave due, so she travelled down the very next day on the milk train from Kendall. When she arrived, Jeger pored through her documentation while firing questions at her: 'Don't you belong to the Labour Party? Do you belong to any political party? What are your family's politics?' Lillian answered truthfully that her family had no political affiliations. He then asked her to explain why she had written 'politically disinterested' on her application form. 'Well, I've never heard of any organisation employing nurses that wanted nurses who were politically minded,' she replied. Then, to Jeger's obvious amusement, she added that 'religion and politics are, like sex in hospitals, never discussed.'

What Lillian did not realise at that point was that politics, far from being taboo, played a fundamental role in the SMAC and its work in Spain, as the Communist Party members of the unit strove to control its activities. Some of the non-Party members complained about the unacceptable 'obsession for political manoeuvering and intrigue' within what was supposed to be a humanitarian enterprise.[15] Furthermore, as Buchanan points out, 'the intensely political environment in which they worked impinged on all of the medical personnel.'[16] Despite her attempts to remain on the margin of any such political conspiracy, Lillian would find herself drawn into it.

Though impressed by Lillian's qualifications and the testimonies as to her nursing knowledge and skills, Jeger pointed out that she lacked experience. 'Well, there's going to be a war,' she countered, 'and I need experience, don't I? And I need it now.'[17] Her determination appeared to convince Jeger, who instructed her to return to work, but not to give in her notice until she heard from him again. However, after another several months of hearing nothing, she wrote to the SMAC yet again. This time, she was told to be ready to go to Spain at a moment's notice, and that she would receive through the post ampoules of anti-typhoid and anti-typhus serum that she had to have before travelling. So, she gave in her notice immediately. She had three weeks' leave due but the sisters who ran the nursing home refused to allow her to take it and they threatened her with all manner of reprisals should she leave them. They also refused to pay her the uniform allowance that was overdue and confiscated from her bedroom the phials of serum that she had been sent.

Thankfully, one of the doctors who attended the home, Dr Hudson, a Quaker, saw Lillian's plight and determined to help her. He approached the local health authorities on her behalf, obtained the sera and gave her the injections. Although all the vaccinations made her quite poorly, the sisters refused to allow her to take even a few hours off duty.

Chapter Three:
Lillian sets out for Spain

Eventually, in June 1937, at the age of just nineteen, Lillian Urmston set out for Spain. Her first port of call was the SMAC's London headquarters. They were also awaiting the arrival of Australian nurse, Dorothy Low, so Lillian was instructed to find modest accommodation at the expense of the Committee. 'Near to the site of what is now London University, Torrington Square, I found a very nice landlady and shacked up with her for nearly a week,' declares Lillian. She and Dorothy met only on the day of their departure for Spain. Nobody accompanied them and (unlike the multitudinous 'farewell committee' present at the departure of the previous group) nobody saw them off, nor were they given any medical supplies or such like to take. Ladened with assorted provisions and first aid kits that they themselves had managed to acquire, they travelled together over land and sea by train and ferry. (Lillian would carry the very same medical kit with her through the Second World War.) The young women travelled through France, changing at Paris and Lyons and then going on to Port Bou. On the train to Paris, their Red Cross armlets attracted the attention of a Swiss student with whom they struck up conversation. They told him that they were going out to work as nurses in the Spanish Civil War. The Spanish Government needed all the help that they could get, they explained, and they were taking out all the medical provisions they had managed to scrounge.

The student told them that he had left the French university at which he had been studying because he had been recalled to do his military training. He explained about conscription in Switzerland and they, in turn, told him about their imminent mission in Spain. He was so impressed by the two young women that by the time they reached Paris he had opened his suitcase and handed them his impressive collection of stamps. 'If you can sell these,' he said, 'I hope you buy a medical kit to take with you.'

The women missed their train in Perpignan but managed to sell the stamps there. They went into a pharmacy and asked if they could exchange them for medical equipment to take with them to Spain. The pharmacist, greatly moved by what he had just heard, went out into the street and told all the passers-by, whereupon a crowd gathered and started cheering. 'We had no idea of the value of the stamps,' admits Lillian, 'but a well-dressed man came forward and handed us a sheaf of notes and said that he hoped that it would also buy us dinner.' Loaded with supplies, they arrived in Port Bou and were promptly detained by the authorities. They had valid passports and visas for Republican Spain, but their arrival was apparently not expected.

> I suppose it was the fact that we didn't go in a flamboyant truck or an ambulance or something—we were just two people with rucksacks. We had been told to travel in navy blue skirts and blouses that were easily washable and to take just a change of light clothing. That was all. We didn't have suitcases or anything and we were put in prison after a lot of arguing. I spoke a little French from school days, but not enough, and certainly only a few words of Spanish and the dictionary I had. And we were taken upstairs in a very cheap type of hotel with no furniture in it except wire beds and iron bed frames—no mattresses or blankets or anything.[1]

They felt tired, hungry, and abandoned. It was not until after several hours that they were eventually taken out, under guard, to a restaurant. By fortunate coincidence, there they saw two men who they thought looked British and, after a brief exchange, they learned that one of them was the lorry driver who had been sent to pick them up. His lorry had broken down on the way and now he was keen to stay a night or two in Port Bou, as he could get easily into France from the town and treat himself to little luxuries that could no longer be obtained in Spain; so he paid for Lillian and Dorothy's train tickets. Thus, after being detained for about seven hours, the women were finally on their way again.

They got to Barcelona in the middle of a blackout and bombing. There was no one to meet them, but they managed to get to the SMAC flat where they were given a far from friendly welcome by Rosita Davson.[2] Lillian remembers the event with some displeasure:

> She never had much time for nurses, I don't think. She wanted us to travel that same night. We had been sitting up in a train for two nights, so we remonstrated, so she took us out. We went to a people's restaurant and then, above all places, instead of letting us have a good night's rest, we were taken to a third-rate cabaret, but there were a number of International Brigaders on leave. They wanted to know who we were, where we were going, and we were told that we would be going to the Aragon front. So, we didn't have much sleep that night—about three hours—and first thing the next morning some men came— the International Brigaders.

The Brigaders escorted the young nurses to the railway station and made sure they were put on the right train. It was a troop train, and they were looked after magnificently by the Spanish soldiers with whom they travelled all the way to the Aragon front. The journey involved several changes of trains and at every station crowds of people cheered and the troops answered them with equal excitement. 'We picked up enough Spanish to know that they were saying, 'We've got foreign nurses with us—they're English!'' explained Lillian, 'and people kept coming and gaping at us and giving us the clenched fist salute. And people were handing us mugs of tea and glasses of drink and sweet buns.'

It took nearly 48 hours to get to the Aragon front, with frequent stops along the way, often to avoid being caught in bombing and shellfire. Another complication was the lack of toilets on the train and the young women quickly learned the knack of jumping off the train, shouting, '*un momento!*' and quickly diving behind a wall or other such obstacle that offered any kind of privacy.

The first British hospital had been established in the outskirts of the town of Grañén, Huesca, near where the Thaelmann Centuria was then based.[3] The town, an anarchist stronghold, enjoyed excellent road, rail and river communications and was close to the active Huesca front. It had suffered armed conflict but had remained in Republican territory. A small, bombed farmhouse was the site chosen for the hospital. It had taken a great deal of hard work to get the dirty and dilapidated buildings into a state of acceptable cleanliness, especially as there was no running water and an almost useless drainage system. The entire team—doctors, nurses, drivers and other assistants spent several days sweeping, scrubbing and mopping, with water brought from the river four miles away, in order to transform the premises into a hospital. Lillian points out that while the appropriate standards of discipline and respect were maintained, the traditional hierarchical divisions in British medicine disappeared, to some extent, in wartime Spain. Doctors not only had to work in specialized fields outside their previous experience, but also to drive ambulances, to organise, and even to clean, their own hospitals. Ambulance drivers had to work as mechanics and general labourers. They were also occasionally called upon to serve as anaesthetists, in an emergency, and were given the task of disposing of amputated limbs. As Lillian would soon learn, nurses performed minor operations, acted as administrators, and made critical decisions about treatment.

The upper floor of the Grañén hospital was used for staff accommodation—that is, two dormitories with mattresses on the floor, separated into male and female sections by a strategically placed curtain. The medical personnel became adept at living and working in primitive conditions. Eventually, as well as a reception or triage area for the classification of wounds, and two operating theatres, the hospital could boast three surgical wards (including one for venereal diseases) offering a total of 40 beds (70 in a state of emergency). During the first month, 118 cases were dealt with. By November, that figure had risen to 1,523 cases and the ambulances had covered a collective total of 14,000 miles.

Like Lillian, several other volunteers would join the SMAC unit during the course of the conflict. One of these was Dr Reginald (Reg or Reggie) Saxton. He had been on holiday in Russia when the first unit went out to Spain and arrived at Grañén in September of 1936, just as the activity on the Aragon front had begun to ease, so his medical work, at that time, amounted largely to that of general practitioner for refugees in the village. He would become responsible for the crucial task of blood transfusion during the coming months, a task with which Lillian was also involved during her early days in Spain.

Due to localized political unrest, in March 1937, during the Quinto-Belchite offensive, the SMAC unit was obliged to leave the Grañén hospital in the hands of the resident anarchist column and move about 12 kilometres south to Poleñino, a town where sympathies still lay with the socialists of the Partido Socialista Unificado de Cataluña (PSUC). Here, they established a hospital in the *Casa del Pueblo*, under the leadership of Spanish surgeon Gonzalo Aguiló Mercader, Provisional Medical Captain of the 27th Division. This was where Lillian and Dorothy were headed. When they finally reached the Poleñino hospital, it was full to overflowing with patients and they set to work almost immediately alongside other British nurses, Patience Darton, Ruth Ormesby, Margaret Powell, and Susan Sutor. Lillian describes the conditions:

We were doing operations because wounds were being infected and having to be reopened. There was no such thing as antibiotics. We were very lucky indeed to have sulphur drugs. The orderlies were in the process of being trained. Besides the doctors we had, we had one Spanish doctor (Aguiló) and a *practicante*.[4] He came from a very good kind of Barcelona family. His training was interrupted but he was excellent as a theatre assistant. He used to give the anaesthetic. We used a great big attic room because it gave most light from all of the windows and we had three operating tables going strong. The equipment was all from England. It had been supplied as a unit by the Spanish Medical Aid, including the ambulance and two trucks.[5]

During the initial stages of the uprising, the British medical unit functioned as a completely independent body, administering emergency medical aid to Republican soldiers. However, by November 1936, the Aragon front was no longer active, the pivotal battles of the war being fought around Madrid. The British volunteers were dealing chiefly with accidents and illness among the local community, while Margaret Powell acted as midwife. It had become clear to the Unit that if it was to continue to provide a valuable contribution to the Republican Medical Service it would have to move to where it could be most usefully deployed. The International Brigades were being formed and most of the medical unit's members believed that it, too, should become part of the Republic's organised army.[6]

Once this was sanctioned by the Committee in London, the Unit went to Albacete, the base of the International Brigade's headquarters in Spain where the thousands of volunteers received their initial training and official indoctrination. In January 1937, the British unit became integrated into the Medical Service of the International Brigades, as part of the *Servicio Sanitario de la República*. Now, along with volunteer soldiers, the medical personnel—

both men and women—would all be subject to the same stringent military rule.

The Medical Service of the Republican Army

The Spanish Civil War saw the first large-scale aerial bombardment of civilian populations as the Germans and Italians used Spain to test their new weapons of mass destruction. More powerful bombs and artillery caused more serious wounds than those dealt with earlier wars and, consequently, innovative methods had to be devised to treat them. Notable advances were made in several areas. Moreover, many of these advances became crucial just a year or so later, in the treatment of casualties among both soldiers and civilians during the Second World War. The four main areas in which medical science advanced during the Spanish Civil War were the organisation of medical support to the armed forces, including the strategic positioning of medical facilities, from front line aid posts and hospitals to rearguard convalescent centres; the development of new surgical techniques for trauma wounds; the control of infectious diseases and the creation and development of blood banks.

Developments in trauma care included the treatment of head and abdominal injuries previously seen as 'hopeless' cases; and the healing of compound fractures of the limbs, previously associated with appalling rates of gas gangrene, leading to amputation and often death.[7] This was based on the closed treatment for fractures associated with Catalan surgeon, Josep Trueta. Such treatment was enabled by the systematic use, in front line hospitals, of bottled blood collected from civilian donors. The creation and development of blood banks for transfusions was of major importance both during and after the war, later proving of vital significance to both military and general medical practice. Greater understanding was also gained of shock as a complicating factor in surgery, with subsequent improvements made in its treatment. Advances were also made in the control of infectious diseases. As we shall see, in her capacity as front-line nurse, Lillian Urmston was involved in most, if not all, aspects of this care and, after her return from Spain on the eve of the Second World War, her knowledge and expertise were highly sought after.

The Republican government had to begin almost from scratch in the creation of a military medical service as the greater part of the existing Army Medical Service joined the insurgent forces. Nevertheless, thanks to the many international volunteers, the new Republican Medical Service was able to draw on the experiences of over two hundred doctors, many of whom had previous military experience in the War of 1914 to 1918 or in conscripted continental armies. By the end of 1937, there were more than 240 doctors and 203 nurses working for the Republican Medical Service.[8]

It soon became apparent that the medical resources of the Republican army were not adequate to deal with the vast numbers of wounded International Brigaders. Furthermore, establishing combat units according to their nationalities and languages called for the creation and designation of medical teams of corresponding nationalities. The International Brigaders were now fighting not only in Madrid but also in Andalusia and Teruel, and their wounded were scattered around the Republican zone in different hospitals. Far from their compatriots, with no news of them and unable to communicate with the medical personnel in whose care they found themselves, these men felt isolated and abandoned. The International Brigades were in need of their own medical service that would take care of wounded Brigaders during their convalescence and later transport them back to the front or, when necessary, take care of their repatriation.

Subject to the orders of the Ministry of War, the Headquarters of the International Brigades Medical Services (*Jefatura de Sanidad de las Brigadas Internacionales*) was established in Albacete under the direction of the French doctor Pierre Roquès, together with doctors Hans Kalmanovic, and Rudolf Neumann (Yugoslav and German, respectively). Dr Neumann later gave a revealing account of the initial days:

> None of us knew anything about military medicine. However, we had to quickly create a Medical Service that would be responsible for the life and health of a growing army of volunteers that would soon consist of 30,000 men. With military hospitals in the rearguard, and on the front line, its own system of transport, the prevention of epidemics, the questions of clothes and food for the troops—all these were problems that had to be solved rapidly. We shared out among us the few books on military medicine that we had brought. Each of us was responsible for a chapter. And we sat on boxes, suitcases, still not unpacked, and we gave talks to each other, we studied![9]

The combined International Brigade Medical Service (*Servicio Sanitario Internacional* (*SSI*)) was led by a Chief Medical Officer, the Bulgarian doctor, Zvetan Angelov Kristanov, known in Spain as Oskar Telge.[10] The International Brigades Medical Services was officially recognised at the beginning of April 1937, shortly before Lillian Urmston arrived in Spain. The British SMAC Unit became part of the International Brigades' Medical Service and, as such, was subject to the command of the *Servicio Sanitario de la República*. The military medical organisation would grow steadily to meet the particular situations and challenges encountered. '[W]e witnessed the birth of a new military medical service and watched it grow from infancy to flourishing maturity under conditions of total war,' states Dr Douglas Jolly.[11]

The organisation of frontline medical facilities: the mobile hospital

The organisation of medical assistance developed during previous conflicts was of limited use in Spain. In earlier wars, after receiving emergency attention at the Battalion First Aid Post, the wounded were evacuated as far as possible from the front (out of artillery range) and treated in previously established rearguard hospitals. As transport was usually slow and difficult, this delayed the surgical intervention required, with a consequent increase in mortality rates. In Spain, efficient methods had to be improvised for dealing with the wounded in action and for handling heavy casualties from constantly shifting battlefronts. Here, it was demonstrated that the reduction of the time-lag between the sustaining of a wound and its subsequent treatment was a crucial factor in saving the lives of seriously injured men and, in less serious cases, in reducing the period of the soldier's military ineffectiveness. This necessitated reorganisation throughout the system of Forward Hospitals and Casualty Classification Centres.

Towards the end of March 1937, some weeks before Lillian Urmston's arrival in Spain, the Republic won its first major victory of the war when it crushed the Nationalist offensive at Guadalajara. The British medical personnel returned to the base hospital at Torrelodones, where they were paid a visit by Oskar Telge, the Head of the Medical Services of the International Brigades. Although buoyed by the victory, Telge was concerned by the rather worrying medical results obtained during the recent battles and was considering a reorganisation of the Republican Medical Service, for which he sought the collaboration of his most experienced doctors, including British trauma surgeon, Alexander Tudor Hart and Catalan, Moisès Broggi. Particularly worrying was the almost total mortality rate of casualties with abdominal wounds or open fractures, and by the frequently fatal infection of wounds.[12] The team explained to Telge that taking the gravely wounded to Madrid, often over difficult roads, undoubtedly contributed to the poor results obtained, especially with cases of intestinal wounds or fractures of the extremities. Emergency hospitals had to be placed near the front, out of sight and, as far as was possible, outside the enemy's firing range. They must be capable of being set-up and dismantled in a short space of time, and moved to where their services were most required, depending on the movements of troops and the positioning of the battlefronts. In a war with so much movement and constantly changing fronts, this would be logistically very difficult to achieve, especially as they would have to be hospitals fully equipped with operating theatres, x-ray machines, materials to make plaster casts, efficient methods of sterilisation and lighting systems and so on. The physicians suggested that a special vehicle be sought in which to house such a mobile hospital. Telge promised he would do all within his power to put the team's suggestions into practice, informing them shortly afterwards that he had commissioned Renault of Paris to build such a vehicle.

The first of these mobile hospitals or *autochirs* arrived towards the end of June. Built into the forward end of the truck (against the wall behind the driver's seat) were an autoclave and a *poupinelle* (a copper oven for the dry sterilization of instruments). These were operated by primus-type burners. Along each side were deep cupboards with sliding doors for the accommodation of instrument boxes, sterilizing drums for linen, and all the equipment necessary for the functioning of an operating theatre. These cupboards had individual straps attached to the wall, for the securing of drums and boxes when the unit was in transit. When the unit was travelling, the space on the floor of the truck was occupied by the furnishings of the operating theatre—two operating tables, folding metal instrument and swab tables, folding metal chairs, a mobile lamp-standard, heating stoves (paraffin and electric) and panniers for supplies, plaster bandages, etc. A Böhler axis-traction frame, for plaster immobilization of fractures in extension, also formed part of the equipment. Even a small sewing machine and washing machine were carried. Lighting was provided by a special 300 watt medical lamp which, when in use, was mounted on a wheeled and counter-weighted standard. This was powered by a small portable electric lighting motor capable of giving about 1,000 watts at 120 volts. A small single-stroke motorcycle engine was usually used for this purpose. In addition, the unit was provided with a motor-car battery and a headlamp for use in those moments between the failure of the lighting motor and its sputtering into activity again. Each unit also carried a refrigerator for the storage of conserved blood at low temperature.

Similar vehicles were specially built or converted and donated to the Republican army from various sources. SMAC volunteer Charlie Innocent drove out to Spain a three-ton truck carrying food, blankets and other supplies from England. He took charge of one of the first *autochirs* to be sent out from London—a converted Bedford furniture van. Charlie was soon to discover that the job of driver of these mobile hospitals often entailed rather more than might initially have been expected. He was responsible for the driving and maintenance of the vehicle as well as the sterilizing of the surgical instruments. In Teruel, in the winter of 1937, he found himself assisting in operations. It was freezing and many of the wounded suffered frostbite and gangrene due to prolonged exposure to the elements before reaching the hospital. Charlie had the grueling task of holding limbs during amputations.[13] Lillian Urmston describes the *autochir* in which she worked:

> The mobile theatre consisted of a large, specially equipped
> ambulance to which was sometimes attached a trailer.
> Inside were fitted shelves and cupboards, complete with

drums, instruments, gowns, gloves, drugs, equipment of ampoules of glucosade or saline for intravenous and intramuscular injections, and anything else necessary for any type of operation and for shock treatment. At the front of the ambulance was a geyser, taps and wash-bowl, and besides this was the autoclave and the usual apparatus for sterilizing. Attached to this 'autochir' would be the surgeon and his assistant, usually a medical student. With them would be a trained nurse and she would probably have two or three male orderlies. One of these might have been specially trained in the use of anaesthetics, for the giving of anaesthetics was included in our nursing duties. [14]

Each mobile team was regarded as a fixed entity that could be moved about within the tactical unit of the army or transferred to another tactical unit. The personnel comprised one chief surgeon, one assistant surgeon, two anaesthetists, two theatre nurses or orderlies, two orderlies, two driver-sterilizers, one electrician and two ward nurses or orderlies. This was the ideal but in conditions of war such ideals were not always achievable. The mobile surgical unit was, for purposes of internal organisation, under the control of the surgeon at the head of the unit. For tactical purposes, however, control was in the hands of the Medical Officer commanding the tactical unit within which the surgical team was working at the time. On most occasions, Forward Hospitals were formed by the Corps Hospital Sections, incorporating mobile surgical units as required for a particular task, the partnership dissolving when the occasion was over. Thus, the mobile surgical unit was tactically a great asset to the Republican Military Medical Service.

The results of the changes made were spectacular, above all in the case of abdominal wounds, where the mortality rate had been almost 100%. Now, a survival rate of 50% was achieved. Considerable improvements were also made in the treatment of fracture cases, thanks to the immediate attention given and the application of new methods of treatment. This was the 'closed method' of treating fracture wounds, as developed by the Canadian surgeon, Winnet Orr, towards the end of the 1914–1918 war. This system combined the radical debridement of damaged tissue around the wound (developed by the German surgeon, Friedrich in 1898), and the subsequent 'closed' healing of the wound in an immobilizing plaster cast, practices which considerably reduced the risk of infection. It was first applied in Spain by Bastos Ansart whose work was studied by the majority of Spanish surgeons who, in turn, adopted it as standard practice during the Spanish Civil War.[15] Many surgeons including Jimeno Vidal, D'Harcourt and Aguilar used this technique but it was the Catalan, Josep Trueta i Raspall, who employed it rigorously and later promoted its use in Spain and England, leading some to attribute Trueta with its actual discovery.[16]

The self-sufficient mobile surgical unit formed the basis of the new 'Three-Point Forward System' of medical provision at the front.[17] Number One Hospitals (emergency Hospitals also known as *hospitales de sangre* or 'bloody hospitals') dealt with the gravely wounded and were placed much nearer the front line than had previously been considered viable, so that the time-lag before surgical intervention could be reduced to under five hours. During the earlier days of the conflict, *hospitales de sangre* were established in villages near the front line and near main evacuation roads. Schools, churches, and other large buildings were used for the purpose. As the war went on, however, and buildings became less readily available, medical teams resorted to creating hospitals in all manner of spaces, including huts, tents, and even railway tunnels. Special Casualty Classification Posts, with trained medical personnel, were set up in advance of these hospitals with a rapid ambulance evacuation service between the two. Number One Hospitals treated wounds with severe haemorrhages, including all those where a tourniquet had been applied, abdominal wounds, severe chest wounds, some head wounds and any cases in which there was gross destruction of tissue or grave shock. The No. 2 Hospital, for the treatment of less serious injuries, would be further away from the front. Trivial cases were passed directly to the sector's Evacuation Hospital.

Chapter Four:
Establishing the frontline hospital –
the role of the nurse

The system had begun to function by the time Lillian Urmston arrived in Spain. She notes that front line hospitals were usually about 6 to 12 kilometres behind the front lines, and second line hospitals at a distance of about 30-40 kilometres. Base hospitals were located at 50 kilometres or more. Whenever possible, these posts were outside the nearest village. There could be up to four posts on the outskirts of larger towns.[1] Doug Jolly, the New Zealand surgeon alongside whom Lillian worked, was a great advocate of the system. He explained that in the earliest days of the war, before bombing planes became much more widely employed, field hospitals were usually located some distance further behind the line than at the end of the war. When air-bombardment became widespread, it proved just as easy to place the hospital near the line as further back. Therefore, there was a steady reduction of the time-lag before surgical intervention as the medical facilities were placed further forward.[2]

The assortment of different places used for these medical facilities invariably required thorough cleaning, but soap and disinfectants, and even water, were usually in short supply. Lillian explains that 'with extreme tact, we had to set an example by starting to clean the chosen building, so that our untrained helpers would realise just how important it was'. Until there were designated officers responsible for the hygiene of a unit, it often fell to the nurse to approach orderlies about the making of sanitary arrangements. 'This was a delicate job,' explains Lillian, 'because more often than not it was performed by those under arrest for some petty misdemeanour'.[3] Lillian describes the conditions in the first

first-aid post in which she worked, in June 1937.

> Owing to a shortage of disinfectants and a general lack of material, we had to clean the place as best we could using cold water, toilet soap and dried straw fastened round twigs which served as mops. A small kitchen, which is always a necessary part of a first aid post, was put in a small lean-to shed in the back yard. There was only sufficient space for fifteen stretchers, and these were placed with the heads against the walls. In one corner of the room near the door was a desk and shelves. Here, the secretary and his assistant worked. Their work was to identify the patient and write particulars in a special book. On the opposite side of the room, placed midway between the line of stretchers, was a large table on which everything necessary for treatment was placed.[4]

In addition to supplies of dressings and splints, antiseptics, and bandages, Lillian notes that stocks included 'coaguline, camphor in oil, morphia, Novocain, stovaine, adrenalin, caffeine, thrombyl, cardiazol (or equivalent), strychnine, anti-tetanic serum, anti-gas serum, codeine pills and hydrogen peroxide'. In the absence of such aids as 'dangerous drug books', she explains, extreme care was taken in the administration of medications. The trained nurse in charge, together with the doctor, was responsible for ordering and giving most of the injections, as well as taking charge of and replenishing the stock.

Prompt and accurate classification of the wounded (or *triage*) was the key to the success of the system. Only when this was carried out could the casualties reach the corresponding hospital and adequate treatment be administered. This vital function had to be carried out by someone with excellent medical knowledge and organisational skills—preferably an experienced doctor. Lillian explains her part in the procedure:

We examined and classified the wounds and I, aided by one well-trained orderly, four assistants and four stretcher-bearers, was responsible for everything else, including shock treatment. After examination, particulars were written down in each patient's note sheet. Later, *all* treatment given was written down so that when the case arrived at the hospital the attendant would know what treatment had been given and when. A coloured tag would also be fastened on the patient's wrist or forehead: red for extreme urgency, yellow for secondary importance, and blue for not so urgent cases.[5]

After emergency attention, all cases of abdominal wounds, lung injuries and certain types of head injuries, as well as those requiring amputation of limbs, were sent to a front-line hospital. Others, including some serious cases but who were not suffering from severe shock, would be sent to a second line hospital. All efforts were made to avoid unnecessary duplication of dressing posts between the front line and the first point of surgical intervention. Thus, the wounded could receive the required attention without undue delay and repeated and unnecessary changing of dressings, etc. Treatments administered at the Classification Post included tetanus and anti-gas gangrene injections, blood transfusion, application or revision of splints and tourniquets, minor surgery and stitching. 'My orderly would give each wounded case an intramuscular injection of 10cc of anti-gas gangrene serum', explains Lillian, 'while the other assistants helped the doctor, replaced dressings, gave strong coffee to the lightly wounded, and reported to me those who were haemorrhaging or who had tourniquets on their limbs.'[6] Writing after the war, she described the work of the nurse:

On taking up front line work in Spain I quickly realized that great things were expected of an English trained nurse. Quite frequently a nurse had not only to sterilize and sort the instruments, but 'dress' the surgeon and his assistants, keep them supplied with swabs, help the anaesthetist, if he was not well experienced, and give intramuscular salines to the patient being operated on. The nurse, therefore, had to be adaptable, able to use every bit of her training experience for the benefit of the patient and the help of the surgeon, who frequently had to perform the most delicate of operations, working against time, and often operating days and nights with very little sleep.[7]

She later adds that owing to a lack of trained medical personnel, the nurse was also expected to carry out methods of treatment that would normally only be carried out by doctors. These included the prolonged treatment of shock by intravenous injections and, of even greater significance, performing blood transfusions.[8] (More of which, presently).

One of the greatest challenges for the nurse was to keep patients warm, as there were never sufficient supplies of blankets, and often little other form of heating. Stoves or wood fires were a rare luxury. Lillian does remember, however, obtaining an oil stove—a prized addition to the hospital equipment. It not only served to warm the wards but was invaluable for quickly heating water for hot water bottles and blood ampoules, and also sterilising instruments. 'Incidentally,' adds Lillian, 'tea was not much used in Spain [...] but wherever an English nurse worked one would be sure to see a stove in use, providing endless cups of tea for patients and staff alike.' Indeed, surgeon Moisès Broggi makes mention of this in his Civil War memoir. Not only does he praise the medical competence of his British theatre nurse, Thora Silverthorne, but also her knack of providing the team with a cup of tea when most needed—during hours of uninterrupted surgery, for example, when the surgeon was battling to stay awake.[9]

Another last-ditch method the nurses used to heat a ward or shock room was to pour a little alcohol into a bowl, then drop into it a lighted piece of paper. The modest heat generated was still greatly appreciated, especially when hospitals had been set up in caves, tunnels, and tents. Lillian was at pains to point out that the bowls of alcohol were never placed near a patient, but in the middle of the room and well away from any table holding bottles of inflammable fluids.[10]

The evacuation service was also of crucial importance to the success of medical provision during the Spanish Civil War. Firstly, as close as possible to the front line, was the Battalion Aid Post to which company and battalion stretcher-bearers brought the wounded from the field. This unit was commanded by the Battalion Medical Officer, usually a captain or lieutenant, with an assistant MO, one or two *practicantes* and stretcher-bearers. As Lillian reveals, however, later on in the war this became impossible as most villages near to the front were demolished. Outbuildings, sheds and, where necessary, tents were used, as well as caves and tunnels. There were some railway tunnels so near to the front that they could not be used for military transport. These would often be converted into bomb-proof field hospitals. Boarding was laid on top of the railway tracks or, where this was unavailable, gravel or rubble would be used. There would be a reception space, a cordoned-off section for the operating theatre and, beyond that, the 'ward' or bed space which, in the larger tunnels, could house up to 150 beds. Walls were whitewashed or otherwise disinfected. Where possible, there would be space left at both ends of the tunnel for ambulances to approach and unload under cover.

After the SMAC unit became integrated into the Medical Service of the International Brigades, they received orders to move. Some of the British nurses remained with the Spanish doctor, Aguiló, and were sent up to the north side of the Ebro as a mobile ambulance unit. Lillian Urmston and Patience Darton were assigned to the medical unit of the 35th Division, under the leadership of Len Crome. They received orders to move southwards, towards the town of Belchite.

When the medical service of a division received orders to

move to another section of the front, they had to dismantle the current hospital or medical post and pack all the equipment, and themselves, into whatever lorries, cars and ambulances were available to the unit, preferably within four hours. Moves were usually made under the cover of darkness and driving without lights over rough, uneven roads meant that travelling was necessarily slow. The convoy was sometimes halted if an air-raid signal was given, and personnel would run for any available cover in the surrounding fields. 'To add to the general discomfort,' states Lillian, 'there were usually about 15 of us sitting on top of a lorry loaded with mattresses.' She also recalls the traffic jams that caused delays. 'During offensives,' she explains, 'troops were always being rushed by lorries or buses to other sections, and this meant that we had to be doubly on the lookout for signs of enemy planes.'[11] She describes a typical move:

> After travelling from 6.30am until 2.15pm without any food or drink, we arrived at the small village of G_____ . We commandeered a huge army hut and set about cleaning it. Luckily, a river flowed nearby, so we had no difficulty in obtaining water, and in a short time, a hospital had been prepared.
>
> One corner of the hut had been curtained off and made into two operating theatres and a 'shock' room. The rest of the hut held 44 beds and two improvised tables on which were placed all the necessary articles of equipment.
>
> Suddenly feeling tired, I decided to stroll across the field, and look at the other hut, which was to serve as sleeping quarters for all the personnel—doctors, nurses, orderlies and chauffeurs. On entering, I noticed our surgeon and his assistant hammering nails into the walls and fastening up screens made of groundsheets and old blankets. I thought it was foolish of him to be doing this instead of obtaining much-needed rest, so moved over to tell him so. He looked up and saw me and then called out: 'Come and see the apartment we have made for you and

the other nurse, so that when you have a chance to sleep you will have greater privacy.[12]

The British volunteers established a hospital at Puebla de Hijar, about 10 miles from the town of Belchite. It consisted of four pavilions or wooden huts, grouped closely together in bleak open countryside. There was neither electric light nor running water. They managed to set up a hospital, but there was no accommodation for the staff, and they ate and slept, when they could snatch the time, out in the open. Lillian recalls: 'We were not in proper buildings, we were on a salient of land that jutted out for about three miles into fascist territory.' The rainy season had just started in Aragon and the Spanish orderlies instructed the medical personnel in the use of camouflage and how to make shelters that were completely waterproof—skills at which they quickly became adept. One of the activities that Lillian remembers was crawling about with buckets collecting snails. These made delicious and nourishing soups and were a welcome means of supplementing the usual ration of *garbanzos* (chickpeas) which were notorious for causing constipation among the unaccustomed British personnel. 'For at least a month we all had swollen abdomens because of the bean diet,' says Lillian, 'there was no bread, no coffee or anything like that'.

Despite the rain, Lillian loved the terrain and the wonderful smell of wild thyme and rosemary that permeated the air. 'The land we were on was glorious,' she declares, 'It would have been perfect in peacetime, for camping, and it gave us a breathing space to get used to the Spanish way of life.' It also gave the British nurses time to dedicate to the training of young Spanish girls as nursing assistants.

Training Spanish nursing assistants (chicas)

Wherever new medical facilities were established, local women would be employed, where possible, in domestic roles and girls would be taken on as much needed nursing assistants. Nursing had become professionalised in Spain by that time and a School of Nursing was established by the Republican Military Medical Service, under the auspices of Dr Planelles, Chief Medical Officer of the 5th Regiment.[13] However, the number of qualified nurses was nowhere near enough to deal with the enormous number of casualties. Thus, the Spanish *chicas* often proved invaluable to the medical teams.[14] Throughout the war, Lillian took an active part in their training:

> Wherever I have worked I have always had to help to train the young Spanish girls to be nurses. They were usually very adept in the practical work, although not so quick in the theoretical side of nursing. Between offensives, when the brigades were resting behind the lines, I sometimes visited them at a doctor's request and gave them lectures on first aid, hygiene, etc. A great deal of patience was required in working with them as they were highly strung and extremely nervous girls. Most of them had experienced bombardments in Barcelona and Madrid, and when bombs fell near our hospitals many of the girls were convinced that we would all be killed.[15]

Nevertheless, she adds, 'whilst we were training them, we found out that they were so anxious to do their stuff. And in no time at all they were helping in the theatre and could do minor operations themselves.' There was one girl in particular that Lillian remembered. She was 16 or 17 years old when her parents were killed as the rebel troops invaded her town. She escaped with the Republicans as they retreated and became part of the militia. When orders were given for female combatants to be withdrawn, she became attached to the Spanish army as an orderly, then eventually joined the medical team.[16]

> Then she caught up with me and she was excellent, and she was good for morale. She was a tiny little thing, Lola, and everyone worshipped her. She was always bright and

gay and it was only when she slept at night that you realized all the tension that was building up in her. She used to have terrible nightmares and when we slept out in the open and we were near to the Nationalist lines we always had to be ready to clap a hand over her mouth when she wakened because she was babbling and screaming with the horror of what had happened in her Andalusian town. I don't think that kid ever got over it.[17]

As work intensified and the availability of trained personnel decreased, the Spanish *chicas* became responsible for medical procedures of increasing complexity. Lillian trained some of them to give intravenous injections. The procedure normally began by heating a 300cc ampoule of glucose saline in a *Bain Marie* while rubber tubing, hypodermic needles, and a pair of dissecting forceps were boiled in a small fish kettle. The *chicas* were instructed to take to the bedside sterile gauze, a bowl of methylated spirit, a little iodine, adhesive plaster, a tube clip, or a pair of artery clips and scissors, a tourniquet, and a receptacle for soiled swabs. Lillian would explain to the girls the importance of rendering everything sterile. When the ampoule of saline was sufficiently heated, she would proceed:

I then held the tip of the ampoule, pressed on a swab of cotton wool against the table edge and filed off the end. Using sterile forceps, I then took the sterilised tubing and needle and attached them to the open end of the ampoule […] One of the girls would hold this and keep the needle wrapped in a sterile swab that had been soaked in alcohol. After filling the other end of the ampoule, I attached this to the rubber tube and pump, after syringing through it a little sterile water. Before taking it to the patient I always 'tried it' to make quite sure that there was no blocking of the tube or needle, and that the solution was not too hot.

After placing the tourniquet in position, Lillian would gently rub the arm or leg to make the vein more pronounced.

This was especially necessary in the case of very shocked patients whose veins were very difficult to place, and who could not help by clenching their fists. When running water was available, the nurse would scrub her hands for three minutes, and then immerse them in alcohol, or any other antiseptic liquid available. Sometimes it was only possible to scrub the hands in a bowl of water and then have alcohol poured over them. Lillian impressed upon her young assistants the vital importance of observing such 'rituals' in primitive conditions.

> One of the girls would thoroughly clean a good-sized area with ether, and, according to the wish of the surgeon for whom I worked, alcohol or iodine would be painted over it. Using forceps, I would take hold of two sterile gauze pads, shake them out, place them on either side of the chosen area, and a third piece over the lower part. (Sometimes owing to extreme shortage of dressings it was impossible to do this.) Then, with my left hand, I took hold of the arm or leg, slightly pressing and pulling down on the skin as I inserted the needle. After doing intravenous injections for a few times, I could 'feel' when the needle entered the vein. When showing the young nurse how to give intravenous salines I would explain how a swelling around where the needle point lay indicated that the needle was not in the vein, and that the fluid was entering the tissues. On loosening the tourniquet, I then regulated the tube clip or artery forceps, and allowed the saline to flow in slowly. This would take about 20 minutes or so.[18]

A swab that had been dipped in iodine was then placed over the puncture and the arm flexed. After two or three minutes the swab was removed, and a small piece of adhesive tape placed over the puncture wound, or the puncture was painted with collodion. The patient's pulse was then carefully noted and charted, and he was monitored for signs of reaction (which were, noted Lillian, 'thankfully rare'). The girls cleared away the used material and carefully washed in cold water the needles and tubes before boiling. Lillian points out that they were eager to gain as much knowledge as possible and were always asking her questions. 'During offensives', she adds, 'when it was necessary to work 30-48 hours without a break, these girls, who were unused to any form of hospital routine, would stay on duty, and work on just as steadfastly as any of us.'[19]

Curiously, Lillian recalls another kind of training received by herself and her nursing colleagues, during her early days in Spain, that is, training in the use of firearms. This contravened the terms of the Geneva Convention and was not something that was generally encouraged. It was certainly not condoned by the SMAC leadership.[20] In Grañén, for example, SMAC administrator, Kenneth Sinclair-Loutit, was alarmed by the actions of British volunteer nurse Bird who took to carrying a pistol 'which I had to ask her to return to its donor,' writes Sinclair-Loutit, 'as the Geneva Convention forbids non-combatants to carry arms.'[21]

Nevertheless, in late 1937, while Lillian was on the Aragon Front near Caspe, she and her medical colleagues were told that they were to be trained in the use of machine guns. They were given lectures by Russian brigaders (whose names were not revealed to them) and they were shown how to strip and reassemble the guns. Lillian confessed that she and the other nurses did not take the exercise seriously until their instructor impressed upon them the gravity of the matter.

This Russian took us out two at a time and he was smart enough to make us competitive because we did treat it as a bit of a lark, and he told us we hadn't got to waste machine gun bullets. I wore glasses and he said to me: 'Do you know behind that farmhouse where we're firing at the haystack, do you know there's some Nationalists stationed there?' I think he was just getting my back up telling me about Nationalists but after that first trial we had two more and I put my finger in that trigger and there were three targets and I systematically went from one to the other and back again, they were great big targets of course, bigger, possibly bigger than a human's body would have been but I knew damn sure that if it was necessary I'd have got a few.[22]

Thankfully, there is no record of it ever being necessary, but Lillian leaves us in no doubt as to how she would respond if it were.

Lillian's équipe had been awaiting orders to move for some time. The rainy season was just coming to an end and the weather was glorious when they were paid a visit by Captain Mark Strauss, Medical Officer of the 15th Brigade, Lincoln Battalion.[23] Strauss and his team were under orders to open a frontline hospital to the northeast, near Quinto in the province of Zaragoza, and were desperate for nurses. With no superior to consult at the time, and considering the exceptional circumstances, Lillian and Dorothy volunteered to accompany Strauss. Lillian recalls that two American nurses in Strauss's team, Esther Silverstein and Irene Goldin, had got lost while coming back from leave and joined them while they were in transit. Lillian was slightly shocked to hear the American nurses address their chief surgeon by his Christian name—something unheard of in British hospitals. Driving through the streets and the outskirts of the ruined town also left a lasting impression on Lillian:

mules and horses and military and civilians and children's bodies were piled as high as five feet, stenched and bloated under the terrific September sun. By the time we got as far as the church they hadn't long cleared out the Nationalist forces who had used that as their base and they had only recently got rid of the last groups of snipers from the belfry. There were more dead people around than living because the Republican policy was to evacuate civilians if possible, not only because of 5th Columnists, but for humanitarian reasons.[24]

Creating and running an operating theatre in such surroundings would be a daunting if not impossible task for which they needed to call on the help and cooperation of the remaining civilians, as Lillian explains: 'So, we got as many women as we could, and they were crying, they had seen their children killed, their other parents bombed and dying of wounds, but they all rallied round and scrubbed with sand and water—that's all we had, we never had enough soap.'[25]

Once the hospital was up and running, work was frenetic, and rest was scarce. 'Sleeping was something—you just came out of theatre and slumped down,' explains Lillian, 'leaned against a wall and just fell asleep until someone shouted: '*triaje, triaje*', meaning go to the casualty bay as we had casualties coming.' Lillian worked as theatre nurse alongside several renowned physicians including Catalan surgeon, Moisès Broggi; New Zealander, Douglas Jolly; British doctor Reg Saxton; and medical student, Gerald Shirlaw (who went by the name of Jerry Steele, in Spain). Broggi recalls that he and his *équipe* were joined at Puebla del Hijar by medical personnel from the Corps of the Army of the East, including some nurses. Broggi remembered, in particular, 'an English nurse named Patience, very distinguished and very beautiful', who joined Tudor Hart's team.[26]

The work was relentless, with 160 operations being carried out in twelve days, in an operating theatre that was little more than a shed. After an epic defence by the Nationalist garrison, the small town of Belchite was eventually taken by Republican forces. Those entering the town spoke of the horrible stench. The hospitals were full of infection and sepsis. The American doctor, William Pike, recorded his first impressions of the fascist hospital they discovered after the battle:

The fascist hospital infirmary was a long, dark, dreary room [...] Eighty wounded fascists had been left there— huddled together like sheep [...] The floor was damp and slimy with blood, foul smelling sputum and vomitus. The air stank of urine and choked your throat with the smell of fetid puss. Every wound was infected. The dressings were hard, rigid, blood-stained [...] tourniquets left on for five-six days. One of the wounded fascists had gone completely mad under the overwhelming load of misery and pain [...] they awoke next day in our light, airy ward-barracks under clean linen.[27]

2. Lillian with Dorothy Low and Spanish driver, Enrique. Lérida, August 1937.

3. From right to left, Lillian, Irene Goldin and Dorothy Rutter, Quinto, October 1937.

4. From right to left, Lillian, Keith (Andy) Andrews, Dorothy Rutter and Leah Manning with British, American and Spanish orderlies, Cedrillas (Teruel).

5. Lillian and driver with ambulance at Cedrillas (Teruel).

6. With American Brigader Norman Dorland, at Alcorisa.
Dorland was wounded at the battle of Brunete at the
end of July 1937, while serving with the XV Brigade.

Chapter Five:
Lillian's involvement in wartime medical advances

Wounds and Infections

The greatest number of cases that Lillian and her colleagues dealt with in Spain were those caused by shrapnel wounds received during bombardments, shellings, or by hand grenades. There were also great numbers of cases of bullet wounds, including those caused by explosive bullets. When asked what the worst kind of wounds were, Lillian replied:

> One cannot say, at sight, if a shrapnel wound is more severe than a bullet wound. There were men with gaping, bleeding shrapnel wounds who recovered quickly after shock treatment; there were men whose sides had been penetrated by bullets which had passed out on the other side, leaving in their wake 14 or even more perforations of the liver, stomach and intestines. This latter type of patient would require shock treatment for as long as six days or more. A small piece of shrapnel would frequently enter an organ and create great internal damage. We did not have a very great number of wounds from explosive bullets, but what there were were ghastly to see. Unless the patient was operated on very quickly indeed, a foam of rapidly spreading gangrene would set in, and the man would be shrieking in agony. On one occasion, while preparations for the operations were in progress, we gave one man an injection of morphia and a large dose (25cc) of anti-gas serum, and the surgeon told me to give him another 25cc a quarter of an hour later. The man was placed on the table and excision was begun. But it was too late and within ten minutes the man was dead.[1]

In Spain, Lillian learned a great deal from the surgeons with whom she worked. These included the New Zealand-born surgeon Douglas Jolly. Jolly had been studying in London at the outbreak of the Spanish Civil War and went out to Spain as a volunteer with the British SMAC. He worked on the front line in every major battle of the war, and made significant contributions to trauma surgery, especially in relation to abdominal injuries. He described these medical innovations in the acclaimed manual *Field Surgery in Total War* which was to become obligatory reading for the Allied medical services in the Second World War.[2] His ability was widely recognized, not least by other prominent members of the SMAC. After working briefly with Jolly in Spain, British nurse Penny Fyvel declared: 'I realised he was the best surgeon with whom I had ever been associated.[3] Alexander Tudor Hart, the surgeon at the head of the British team shared her opinion: 'Jolly was like me, only better', he affirmed. 'He was the best surgeon we had'.[4]

Working alongside Jolly, Lillian gained experience in the treatment of abdominal wounds. Later, during preparations in Britain for the Second World War, she shared that knowledge with the British nursing fraternity, giving lectures in and around the Home Counties and writing a series of articles for the *Nursing Mirror*. Using her experience in Spain, she gave details on how to identify the symptoms of particular conditions; described the treatments administered and what degree of success was achieved. She discussed, for example, the occurrence of peritonitis as a complication of abdominal wounds:

> when peritonitis occurred, the abdomen rapidly became distended and rigid. The pulse was rapid and feeble, respiration quick and shallow, the patient complaining of great thirst and pain. As most of these cases (resulting chiefly from hand grenades) already had drainage tubes in the abdomen, our duty was to concentrate on diluting the toxins. The patient was given water or not, according to

the surgeon's instructions. He often quickly developed all the general signs of toxaemia, including delirium followed by coma, and would be kept under morphia. The nurse would give 300cc of saline intravenously, followed by 300cc or more intramuscularly, every four hours. Where possible, a continuous drip saline apparatus would be used. Frequently, the doctor would order, when available, injections of some anti-septaemic agent. Sometimes cases which had received prompt treatment [...] did recover. [5]

Lillian affirms that a remarkable success rate was also achieved with lung cases. On occasion, even where surgery had been successful, there was the danger of infection.

Where infection occurred, the patient would be flushed and delirious. There was also difficulty in breathing, frequently due to the fact that the patient could not expectorate the mucus which was forming, and usually had consistent pain; he was also unable to sleep. In lung injuries, as in certain head wounds, we gave intravenous injections of hypertonic saline, usually 20cc every six hours. Codeine oils, too, were of great use in soothing the local symptoms.[6]

The irrigation of wounds was usually carried out using boracic lotion (1-25), saline solution, or Dakin's solution, according to what was available. The wound was then dressed using gauze wrung out of a solution of hypertonic saline. Resting the wounded part often involved a degree of improvisation and ingenuity on the part of the medical team. 'In abdominal wounds we usually tied a towel or a broadly folded strip of material round the abdomen,' explains Lillian, while for chest wounds triangular bandages were used, or patients had their chests 'strapped' with adhesive plaster. In the case of limbs, explains Lillian, 'we would improvise all kinds of splints from Kramer wire'.[7]

After lessons learned from the First World War, where a

high percentage of wounds of the extremities led to gas gangrene, preventative treatment for gangrene was administered. Depending on availability, a wounded man would receive 10cc of anti-gas serum at the first-aid post then, upon arriving at a hospital, he would be given another 10cc injection. Immediately after operation, 25—50cc intramuscular injections of anti-gas serum would be given every four to six hours, until 300cc had been administered.[8] Lillian could remember only one case of tetanus in Spain:

> A man, about thirty years of age, was brought from the lines with a fairly superficial shrapnel wound in the abdomen. The surgeon excised the wound edges, irrigated with hot saline solution and sutured the wound. He was not suffering from shock, so merely received the routine treatment, which included the immediate giving of 10cc of anti-tetanic serum, besides the 10cc he had received while in the front-line first-aid station. On the evening of the third day, however, he complained of abdominal pain, a feeling of tightness in the region of his wound and pain in the neck while attempting to move his head from side to side. He was ordered, and immediately I gave him, a 25cc intramuscular injection of anti-tetanic serum. This I gave every two hours. I also stood by with chloroform in case he started with convulsions, but it was not necessary.
>
> After 10 hours, the ATS dosage was increased to 50cc every three hours. After 24 hours no further symptoms had occurred, and the patient was sleeping a little. We gave him fluids, *ad lib*, chiefly condensed milk, because we had no sugar and could not obtain fresh milk. On the sixth day, the patient was evacuated, no longer complaining of pain in the neck or soreness in the abdomen.[9]

Cases received at the front were mainly shrapnel and bullet wounds, while in the rearguard the casualties were mostly from shrapnel. In the small towns and villages, between the front line and the rear guard, as well as wounded soldiers there were frequently civilians with shrapnel wounds. Sometimes, these were refugees who had been strafed by enemy planes while fleeing along the roads. Lillian rarely saw cases of burns from incendiary bombs in Spain, though she does remember the case of a wounded aviator. His aeroplane had been shot down, and the petrol tank had exploded. He suffered deep and extensive wounds to the head, chest, and abdomen, besides multiple fractures and despite the administering of prompt shock treatment, he died within two hours. Another case she remembered was in September 1937, soon after her arrival in Spain. A chauffeur was taken to the hospital after his vehicle had been in a collision. Again, the petrol tank had exploded, and the patient suffered a fractured femur and burns to the hands, lower abdomen, and upper leg. Lillian explains the treatment administered:

He was given an injection of camphor and caffeine, followed a little later by a 300cc intravenous injection of glucoside. He also had an injection of morphia. As he responded very well to this treatment, the surgeon was able, quite soon, to put up his leg in a Böhler splint. As we did not have a gas and oxygen apparatus, we had to use ether for anaesthetic. I thoroughly cleaned the wound with a solution of soap and water, then mopped over the burned area with a swab dipped in methylated spirits and then with ether. We had no tannic acid in any form, so reverted to picric acid (1/2% solution). We soaked strips of gauze in this and laid them lightly over the area. This was bandaged lightly but firmly, using triangular bandage. I cannot say the wounds received the correct, routine treatment. Sometimes the dressings were renewed every three hours, other times, owing to the pressure of work, five hours would elapse before the dressings were renewed. After just more than three weeks, the burns were almost healed. We then applied, twice each day, a dressing which was frequently used in Spain: a special gauze which had been prepared with Vaseline and containing antiseptics and healing properties. I did not look after him until he was cured because he was evacuated, but the doctor came across him about four months afterwards and reported that 'all was well'.[10]

Treatment for haemorrhage and shock

During the first few months of the conflict there were alarming numbers of deaths due to haemorrhage among Republican troops. Dr Joaquín d'Harcourt Got, chief of the Surgical Services of the Republic cites the extreme conditions, the ad hoc provision of medical facilities, and the lack of experience of the practitioners involved. However, rapid and spectacular improvements were made after the consolidation of the combined Republican medical services, with the help of international expertise, together with the work of the Republican Blood Transfusion Service under the direction of Catalan haematologist Frederic Duran i Jordà.[11] Lillian describes the routine adopted in her medical équipe for dealing with haemorrhage:

> In the receiving room, when the doctor had examined the wound, gauze wrung out of adrenalin would be placed on the bleeding area. If patients had tourniquets on their limbs, the orderlies would inform me, and if necessary, after first seeing if the haemorrhage had ceased, I would replace it [...] Cases that showed signs of internal haemorrhage were operated on as quickly as possible.[12]

Most, if not all, severely haemorrhaging patients were in shock. In Spain, the importance of stabilising patients in shock was widely recognized. American surgeon and international volunteer, Sidney Vogel, writes:

> Shock of itself can kill [...] The conditions that bring on shock—pain, privation, cold, hunger, thirst, bleeding—are

the everyday conditions of war [...] And to treat shock, to cure it, becomes to the doctor a symbol of the whole reason and purpose of war medicine. To treat shock, we reverse the process of privation, the everyday process of war. We supply heat, blood by transfusion, we give complete rest and freedom from pain (often by morphine), we prevent further aggravation of the original injury, we attempt to bring the body back to normal. And to do this requires speed, efficiency, organisation.[13]

Lillian gained a great deal of expertise in the treatment of shock. It was, to a greater or lesser degree, usually present in all the cases she dealt with, even those where severe haemorrhage had not taken place.[14] She later explains in detail the kind of treatment administered to those who were suffering from shock. This would begin by calming and reassuring the patient, while using blankets and, where possible, hot water bottles, to raise the body temperature. The feet would also be slightly raised to stimulate the flow of blood to the heart.[15]

In all our severely wounded cases, especially the abdominal ones, it was necessary to give prolonged shock treatment. Usually, 4-5 litres of blood were given in a period of 2-3 days. Besides this, intramuscular injections of saline or a similar preparation would be given, usually, 2.000ccs, each day for the first two or three days, then gradually the amount would be decreased. I found that if frequent intramuscular injections of glucosade were given extreme irritation was raised, sometimes resulting in sloughing of the skin in that particular area.[16]

Also used in the treatment of shock were injections of camphor in oil of 5cc or 10cc, caffeine 2cc. 1cc of adrenalin was given in cases of rigor after blood transfusion. The clotting agent, Coagulin, was given intramuscularly in doses of 10cc or 20cc. When necessary, morphia was also administered.

Lillian explains that when shock was present, the collapse of veins was a common occurrence, making it difficult to insert a needle. The problem was compounded by the lack of suitable needles—those most often available being of a large bore. Even these were a scarce commodity and they had to be sharpened and reused repeatedly, like most other matériel. Lillian notes, for example, that the ampoules of blood from Duran's Barcelona transfusion centre (see below) were always prepared complete with tubing and needle. So, when she had to use an ampoule, she would cut off the tubing, thoroughly clean and sterilize it, and keep it for reuse in future emergencies. Ampoules containing saline and glucoside were fitted in this way.

> We filed the ends of these ampoules and fitted one end with a tube and 'pump' and the other with ordinary fine tubing, to which was attached a needle, either for intravenous or intramuscular, as the case might be. Therefore, if I acquired a number of these, I could place a needle in the situation for an intramuscular injection and carry on with another urgent task.[17]

Blood transfusion

The major obstacle to the practice of blood transfusion was the naturally occurring phenomenon of coagulation, once outside the body. Therefore, historically, direct arm-to-arm methods of transfusion were the most widely used. The discovery of anticoagulants meant that blood could be extracted and then put on one side until needed—of crucial importance during wartime.[18] By the end of the First World War, indirect transfusion with citrated blood was being used by some pioneering surgeons. By the 1930s in Spain, doctors and surgeons were firmly convinced of the therapeutic and surgical value of transfusion, but satisfactory techniques for its administration were still to be developed.[19] Tragically, it was the outbreak of civil war that would prove the definitive impulse to such progress.

As director of the Blood Transfusion Service of the Republican Army, Duran spearheaded wartime blood transfusion therapy and created the first reserves of blood from volunteer donors for military and civilian use. His considerable knowledge and practical expertise also inspired, informed, and ultimately laid the foundations for the provision of blood transfusion in Britain on the eve of the Second World War.

Preserved (citrated) blood had several advantages: it did not clot, it lasted several days before use, if refrigerated, and donors did not have to be found at the moment of need—often in extreme circumstances when time was of the essence. Duran concluded that the only possible way to satisfy the urgent need for massive supplies of blood was to appeal for donors among the civil population.[20] He and his team threw themselves into the complex task they had been set: to obtain blood, test, classify and preserve it and then transport it to the front for eventual transfusion into patients. Thanks to energetic propaganda campaigns, including radio appeals, there was no shortage of volunteers and in less than a month Duran was able to deliver the first batch of bottled blood (a modest seven litres) to the front, thus launching a new era in the history of blood transfusion.

Blood distributed to the front line and base hospitals was chiefly from blood group O (universal), crucial in situations where the blood group of the wounded could not be determined. In order to maximize potential resources, blood donor centres were established in large, densely-populated cities—Barcelona, Madrid, Valencia, and Jaen.

Blood was accepted from healthy individuals between the ages of 18 and 40 who donated at regular periods of not less than three weeks. A reference index was created whereby the details of each donor were recorded in terms of name, address, hematic group and the results of diagnostic tests carried out for tuberculosis, malaria, syphilis and other diseases.[21] By means of cross-indexing, the staff of the Transfusion Service could check exactly when they had taken blood from any given donor, the latter's state of health, etc. By July 1937, 3,000 donors had been registered[22] and by the end of the war there was a bank of 28,900 donors.[23]

Given the conditions at the time, many of the donors were malnourished and care was taken that the act of giving blood should not cause further detriment to their own health. After giving blood, the donors were allowed rest and were given a cup of coffee or a tot of brandy. Where possible, each also received a small quantity of food, such as a packet of rice and a tin of meat or condensed milk, paid for out of funds contributed by relief organisations such as the British SMAC. Donors were also given a permit to purchase extra quantities of staple foodstuffs such as eggs, meat, milk and vegetables. The SMAC was a fervent supporter of the Republican Blood Transfusion Service and, thanks to public donations, it was able to supply it with refrigerators, vehicles, and other equipment, as well as special funds for the blood donors.[24] This support continued throughout the war. In the summer of 1938, during preparations for the battle of the Ebro, Leah Manning pleaded with the SMAC for further help for the Service. 'There can be little doubt that at the moment, this is the most urgent necessity, in Spain on the medical side,' she wrote. Food was now scarce, and people were becoming pre-tubercular. To make sure that blood was not taken from people with tubercle, the Blood Transfusion Service needed an X-Ray apparatus for screening.[25]

Duran developed a transfusion apparatus that prevented the preserved blood from coming into contact with the air, thus enabling transfusion in totally aseptic conditions. This vacuum-sealed tube became known as the 'Auto-injectible Rapide'.[26] The filled tubes were packed individually, each in a cardboard box. Both flask and box were labeled with the particulars of the blood/group/donor/date, etc., and stored in a refrigerator, at no higher than one or two degrees (Centigrade) above zero. This temperature was maintained during the transportation of the blood to the front, using specially adapted trucks (and, later, railway carriages) equipped with refrigerators. Advanced military posts and frontline hospitals were fitted with fridges run on electricity, petrol or paraffin. The first reserves of blood from the Barcelona service were dispatched to the front in a refrigerated van that had been used, before the war, for the delivery of fish.

One of Duran's greatest achievements was the simplification of the transfusion technique, which enabled it to be carried out by any experienced medical auxiliary worker. The pre-packed auto-injectable *Rapide* was ready for use. The apparatus terminated in a hypodermic needle, sterilized and also sealed in glass. Once the seal was broken and the needle inserted into a vein, the blood began to flow as a result of the air-pressure inside the flask. It was much quicker to execute than other techniques, since all the material was sterile, and no additional sterilization was necessary.[27]

Among the most notable of the international volunteers involved in blood transfusion in Spain were celebrated Canadian thoracic surgeon Norman Bethune and British doctor Reginald Saxton. Norman Bethune arrived in Spain in November 1936, at the head of a delegation from the Canadian Committee to Aid Spanish Democracy (CASD). Though his whirlwind stay was fraught with controversy, Bethune made a tremendously significant contribution to the Republican Blood Transfusion Service. After seeing the blood transfusion service of Barcelona in operation under the direction of Dr Duran, Bethune decided to create a similar service in Madrid. Funded by the CASD from donations from the Canadian public and supported by Socorro Rojo Internacional, the institute would be named the *Servicio Canadiense de Transfusión de Sangre* (later, the *Servicio Hispano-Canadiense de Transfusión de Sangre*).

Dr Reg Saxton was with the British medical unit present in the republican defence of Madrid. There were tremendous losses, and wounded flooded into the emergency hospital that the British unit had set up near the front. Reg was in charge of triage, prioritizing the wounded and preparing them for surgery.[28] It was here that he first became seriously concerned about the lack of provision for blood transfusion. Though Reg had some basic knowledge of transfusion techniques and some rudimentary equipment, there was simply not enough blood to give all the necessary transfusions. There were very few local people to draw upon as donors and all members of the medical staff were already giving to their absolute limits. 'We had at that time no transfusion syringes and no satisfactory needles', explains Reg. 'I collected, however, two sets of instruments to enable me to dissect a vein and insert a cannula.'

> I had a long rubber tube and a funnel. So I delivered the blood into the patient by pouring it into a funnel and it came down a tube and it went through a cannula into the patient's vein. And it worked. It worked very well but, of course, it was a bit tedious and troublesome and the sterilizing wasn't too easy or even too perfect. But still, we just had to wash it out and boil it up and do it again. And this is how I was transfusing our severely exsanguinated patients.[29]

From these tentative beginnings, Reg would steadily develop his knowledge and expertise, and would go on to provide a blood transfusion service in all the war's major battles. In the early days, he was given a great deal of help, as well as supplies of blood, from Norman Bethune, director of the blood transfusion service in Madrid. After Bethune's departure from Spain, most blood supplies would come from Duran's service in Barcelona. Reg also set about devising an alternative source for when supplies were short. As well as classifying the blood of all the medical personnel, as potential donors, he also tested that of troops and of the local population where the medical unit was stationed.

Later, Reg acquired a large Ford evacuation ambulance that had been bombed. Its destroyed body was refitted as a laboratory and travelling blood transfusion unit that would enable analyses and transfusions to be carried out near the front lines, where they were most needed. The lab carried all other available means for the treatment of haemorrhage and shock, such as blankets and large numbers of hot water bottles, blocks for raising the foot of the bed, etc.[30] From humble beginnings, the laboratory developed into something much more sophisticated, gradually becoming an integral part of the medical service. Like the *autochir*, the mobile lab could be quickly moved up to the front and begin functioning immediately, without the need to set up equipment from scratch. Reg managed the only self-sufficient, travelling laboratory and transfusion unit in the Republican Medical Service.

Lillian Urmston gives us an enormously valuable insight as to how blood transfusion was carried out on the frontlines during the early days of the war before the work was taken over by doctors and other specially trained individuals. Almost since her arrival in Spain, she had been transfusing preserved citrated blood from Duran's Institute in Barcelona.[31] Even before she came to work alongside Reg Saxton, Lillian was keen to learn as much as she could about transfusion. While working as part of Moisès Broggi's équipe in Puebla del Hijar, she received instruction from the Spanish haematologist who had joined the team.[32] He took her with him to Barcelona where she was given further training in blood transfusion procedures and blood grouping, eventually becoming quite competent at the technique involved in indirect transfusions.[33] After the war, she reflects:

I have always found, personally, that in wartime working under chaotic conditions, the nurses I have known, the well-trained nurses, have always been better at quickly getting into veins than doctors, probably because we had to get used to giving intravenous salines and so on. Therefore, it was much easier for a nurse, in my opinion, to give blood transfusions than it was for the average doctor, and no one disputed it. And it wasn't a case of being told that you were taking charge of a blood transfusion unit or anything like that. In the early days we had no commissars attached to us who would give us orders. We instinctively knew and we would say to the surgeon: 'Suppose I do such a thing?' The surgeon would know by this time what we were capable of, and he would agree, and we all worked in harmony.[34]

Lillian adds that during offensives in Spain it was not always possible to obtain sufficient ampoules of stored blood, and in frontline emergencies, she and her colleagues were frequently called upon to act as donors. One such occasion, during the battle of Teruel, was witnessed by Winifred Bates:

Here is a typical scene. It is the middle of the night, but we have forgotten time. A wood fire burns on the open hearth. The floor of the small room is blocked with stretchers. Phyllis [Hibbert] kneels by a stretcher with a syringe in her hand, and as she does so she glances at the next stretcher. 'Look, that man's dying', she says and darts from the room. Returning at once she gives him an injection and Doctor Saxton follows her in. The donor for the blood transfusion [Lillian Urmston] just sits on the floor. There is no comfort, no elaborate preparation; we must be quick. When it is done he goes out saying to me, 'Get her some coffee, will you?' The cook is bending over the fire where he is keeping hot a pot of soup and a can of coffee in case anyone should have time for food. By the time I have got the coffee the nurse has slipped away and gone on duty in her ward again.[35]

Chapter Six:
Victuals and Visitors

SMAC supplies

Obtaining supplies for both medical and general everyday needs was often very difficult. The established channel was through Rosita Davson, SMAC liaison officer at the transit flat in Barcelona. Davson, a somewhat mysterious figure, was not a particularly popular character with her colleagues and Lillian was no exception.

> I don't think anyone liked her. She never did a good thing for me at all. [...] she never gave me cigarettes to take back to the front. She never gave me a tin of butter or a packet of tea. She was supposed to run the equivalent of a comfort fund for nurses, but I never got anything.

There were, indeed, many complaints about Davson's behaviour. Although describing Davson as 'very welcoming', American volunteer, Monica Milward, declared that she 'gives the impression that it is a personal favour on her part if she gives me anything [...] this is not only my opinion, but that of all the SMAC people'.[1] Later, 'with hindsight' Milward concluded that Davson was 'definitely up to something "irregular".'[2] A frequent complaint was that while the medical teams always experienced great difficulty getting much needed supplies, Davson was allegedly providing those at the British Embassy with little luxuries, despite the fact that they could still get their own supplies and were not in need of help. Some of the SMAC personnel suspected Davson of spying for the British government—suspicions that were deepened after the war, when she became a member of the British Diplomatic Corps.

Lillian recalls that one of those few who managed to make Davson comply with requests was Harry Evans, the head of Transport and Distribution. She describes Evans as 'a superb mechanic, and superb at training Spaniards to keep things on the road,' but Harry evidently had additional skills.

> Periodically, he used to burst into Barcelona and quarrel like mad with Rosita Davson and get supplies out of her. It turns out that she had a storeroom nearby [...]. Nan [Green] said Harry Evans was the champion. He would frighten the hell out of her by threatening to send someone back to England and make 'this that and the other' report on her [...] we would get the stuff, but it always seemed to take a visit to get the things and we knew it wasn't the people in England. The sad thing was that some of my old patients were sending half-a-crown a month by postal order to the Spanish Medical Aid Committee and half-a-crown for a pensioner was a fortune.[3]

Winifred Bates was very critical of Rosita Davson. Winifred and her husband Ralph used their knowledge of Spain and their abilities as writers to help in the government's propaganda and information services.[4] Ralph Bates joined the International Brigades soon after the war broke out, becoming editor of *Volunteers for Liberty,* the journal of the British Fifteenth Brigade. He also spied on International Brigaders for the Communist Party of Great Britain. From December 1936 to July 1937, Winifred worked as a translator and propagandist for the PSUC before becoming propagandist and liaison officer for the SMAC. She had initially sought secretarial and administrative work with the unit, but the job went to Rosita Davson. Bates would later vilify Davson as a 'cruel and objectionable character' who caused internal unrest and divisions amongst the nursing and administrative staff of the SMAC.[5] She even accused her of engaging in acts of sabotage.[6] Leah Manning, on the other hand, was at pains to explain that Davson's role with the SMAC put her in a difficult position and the problems arose because she was merely fulfilling her instructions from the Committee with regard to the distribution of supplies. Manning reported her own efforts to resolve tensions between Davson and some of the SMAC nurses.[7]

On Bates' visits to the varying hospitals, the nurses eventually began to turn to her for advice. In hospitals at home, they could rely on the matron for this kind of support, but here in Spain they were lacking any such figure.[8] 'I decided that what they wanted was a Political Commissar-cum-housekeeper,' declared Bates.[9] So, with the blessing of the SMAC, she took it upon herself to undertake this role. Despite her apparent concern for the nurses in her care, evidence indicates that Bates had a clear political agenda and sent reports to the Communist Party on medical personnel.

The political background of many of the British volunteers in the International Brigades was overwhelmingly Communist,[10] and although the SMAC was not officially created by the Communist Party, many of its founders and volunteers were members of it. However, not all the British medical staff in Spain shared political allegiance to the Communist Party. This irked Bates. In a report to the SMAC about the nurses under her care, she discussed their political backgrounds and her attempts to 'convert' them to communism. Those from Communist backgrounds are showered with praise: Ann Murray was 'a Communist in every way' working well among the Spanish women as well as the English nurses, and Margaret Powell was 'sincere, disciplined, and hard working.'[11] Those who were unsure of their political stance, such as nurse Margaret Finley, were in need of political 'training' to awaken them to the virtues of Communism, while Barbara Briscoe, who appeared to have 'no political ideas at all', needed help from Comrades on the matter, 'when she awakens mentally'.[12] Bates supported those volunteers such as Nan Green and Rosaleen Smythe who shared her firm Communist convictions, and opposed those like Rosita Davson and Lillian Urmston, who did not.

Nurse Molly Murphy (née Morris) and her husband John Thomas ("JT") Murphy were prominent members of the Communist Party of Great Britain (CPGB) during its formative years. However, it was hardly political conviction that prompted Molly to join the Party, as she explains: 'it meant simply that my husband's friends were my friends, his loyalties my loyalties'.[13] When JT was expelled from the party in 1932, Molly resigned. In Spain, she made it clear to those at home that she had got the measure of the members of the British Medical Unit—both the exemplary and the less praiseworthy:

> None of the Party members here have made me have the slightest wish to join the BCP. And it comforts me quite a lot to know that those in our M. U. [Medical Unit] wouldn't have the slightest chance of being members of a well organised CP. [...] with very few exceptions in the M. U. the non-Party people here are far the best and most conscientious in their work.[14]

A similar opinion was held by Sir Richard Rees, volunteer ambulance driver attached to the 35th Medical Division Unit. In his autobiography, *A Theory of my Time*, Rees declares:

> I arrived in Barcelona in April 1937 in a mixed state of exaltation and despair [...] My exaltation sprang from the thought that I was preparing to risk my life for socialism, or the European working class, or something, and my despair from a more down-to-earth appreciation of my motives.'[15]

However, Rees soon became disillusioned with the way the Communist Party of Great Britain was taking control of the British Medical Unit. After six months in Spain, he writes, 'I was beginning to feel that there was no place for me as an organiser, unless I was a Communist or prepared to be a

Communist stooge.'[16] Rees resigned from the medical unit and joined the Quakers' Spanish relief organisation in Barcelona, where he finally felt that he could make a worthwhile contribution:

> any foreigner who was not a Communist was made to feel at best an outsider and at worst a potential victim of the political police. In this shadowy and impalpable but all-pervading reign of terror the business-like Quaker organisation was an oasis of sanity.[17]

Meanwhile, Winifred Bates continued her political mission. She spent time 'teaching' nurse Dorothy Low (Lillian's companion on the journey out to Spain) and eventually managed to 'completely change her political outlook'. However, she had little success with 'our Lillian', who, true to form, refused to be told how to think and act by another. Bates would later exact her vengeance. Bates' Communist friend, Nan Green, got caught up in the political infighting at the convalescent hospital at Valdeganga where she was hospital administrator and she was accused of sexual promiscuity. Bates vehemently defended her, helping her to secure a new post at the hospital in Ulcès and later as secretary to Dr Len Crome, the Chief Medical Officer of the 35th Army Corps'.[18] Her attitude towards Lillian, on the other hand, was at best contradictory, at worst, vindictive. This is her report to the Communist Party:

> Lillian Urmston. Is very brave, reported by the doctors to be a good nurse. Has developed from being nothing at all to being a sure antifascist. I have had several reports about her being undisciplined but have always found her working when I have chanced to visit her hospital. I hesitate to give my opinion on her lest I should be considered prudish and over-English. I have spent some time with her recently and have given serious thought to the remarks I am about to make [...] she objects to any

other International nurse, especially English, working with her. She likes to be the only English person in a village because people make a fuss of her. She never leaves the men alone and makes herself cheap with every man she meets, even in Barcelona. Her behaviour is vulgar and she is a discredit to the British Medical Aid here. I have tried to be patient with her and help her, but I sometimes think that she is too conceited to learn.[19]

This contradicts the opinions of Lillian's conduct and capabilities shared unanimously by her colleagues and superiors. Dr Gerald Shirlaw, for example, worked with her during the Spanish Civil War, and offered the following testimonial to her future employers in Britain:

Nurse Urmston was a member of the British Medical Unit, performing her humanitarian duties as a Sister in many parts of Spain. I am well qualified to speak of her professional abilities as she was connected with me in the 35th Division of the Spanish Army from July 1937 to March 1938, where she was Theatre Sister in various front line hospitals. I have always found her a most capable assistant in all branches of war surgery.

Owing to her extreme capabilities, Nurse Urmston was promoted to the 15th Army Corps, where she was Sister in charge of that Unit and with whom she remained in that capacity until the ultimate days of the war.

I have always found Nurse Urmston to be extremely conscientious in all her work, and she has always enjoyed the popularity of those with whom her work has brought her into contact.[20]

George Jeger also gave Lillian an excellent reference, stating that in the two-and-a-half years spent with the SMAC, she worked in different hospitals on various fronts, 'often under shell fire and bombardment, and in circumstances of great personal danger'. Jeger concludes:

All our reports show her to have been an able and efficient

nurse, with considerable courage and common sense, and popular with all her colleagues and patients. We have no hesitation in recommending her with confidence for any post for which she may be applying.[21]

There is evidence of Lillian's involvement in one relationship of a romantic/sexual nature in Spain. That was with Dutch Brigader, Evert Ruivenkamp. After meeting her while he was a patient at the Ulldemolins hospital, Ruivenkamp described Lillian as 'a damn fine girl'.[22] They became friends and corresponded between Evert's visits to the hospital. On one such visit, he and Lillian helped organise a fiesta for the local children. The following day, he notes in his diary:

> I feel marvelous. We slept together. In reality, we are more than friends. I want us to get married but that is impossible [...] We have our work, right now. Later, when this hell is over, we can talk about that—whether we can live and work here, or whether we can go to the United States.[23]

Unfortunately, there is no record of Lillian's side of the story, nor does she allude to it in her interviews after the war. She was recalled from Ulldemolins at short notice, before the battle of the Ebro, and deployed to the front. She and Ruivenkamp lost touch and he eventually presumed her dead after the letters he sent to Ulldemolins went unanswered.

Parcels from home

Ursula Summerville, Lillian's Quaker friend in Kendal, had told her to write to her if she needed anything sending out to Spain and to give her and her Quaker friends an account of what was going on. After writing two letters without reply, Lillian began receiving regular parcels from the Quakers— sometimes twice a month, if she was stationed in the same area for any length of time. She could not hide the thrill this gave her. 'A great tea chest would arrive with medical equipment, steel, rust-proof surgical equipment, bandages, tins of tea, soup and everything like that—everything!' She even wondered whether they were sending consignments more often and they were being 'pinched', as, she explains, this was not an uncommon occurrence, 'anything that could be stolen was "organised": it disappeared.'

The arrival of a parcel was always the cause of great jubilation, not least because the contents invariably helped to supplement the meagre diet of the patients. 'When carrying out duties near the front lines, a nurse finds that she also has to act in many other capacities,' wrote Lillian, after the war. 'Army cooks, especially when rations of food are neither plentiful nor varied, are not always able to satisfy the whims of a patient. Therefore, a nurse must be prepared to help produce appetising drinks, etc., out of very little'.[24] In this respect, the frequent parcels sent out from England proved invaluable, and were very much appreciated, as Lillian explained:

> when we gave the convalescents coffee to drink, those who needed stimulating, they were crying and I had to explain that the kind of people in England who were sending these things to me personally were just like them—people who worked in cotton mills and iron foundries, ministers and Quakers.'[25]

As Lillian was a non-smoker, hers were probably the only packages that did not contain tobacco. However, observing the generosity of the senders, her colleagues begged her to ask them to send cigarettes. This she eventually did and was more than satisfied with the results. 'I don't think Miss Summerville approved of smoking, but I told her it was for soldiers and after that we got huge consignments and once or twice I got a chest literally full of cigarettes.' Not all the cigarettes were given to the wounded. Lillian explained that they proved excellent bartering currency with farmers, for example, who were unwilling to sell milk, eggs or cheese, or any other produce that would be extremely valuable to the medical unit. 'We used to bribe them, bully them, bargain with them,' explains Lillian, 'and I became very adept at knowing the value of a packet of cigarettes as to how many eggs or milk and so forth we ought to have.' It was mainly the patients who benefitted from such comforts, but, adds Lillian, 'If we felt justified, we would open a little can of milk and have some ourselves, in tea, as a great luxury.'[26]

Lillian recalled a less pleasant event that took place in one busy frontline hospital—the arrival of Soviet Communist, Raisa Moiseevna Azarh. She had studied Medicine at the Institute of Red Professors of the All-Union Communist Party and, unbeknown to Lillian, was a distinguished physician with extensive military medical experience in previous conflicts. In Spain, she was a political commissar and adviser to the *Sanidad Militar*, but Lillian was unimpressed by the visitor:

> when she joined us, we were mad as hell that we were wearing cotton rope sandals, no stockings, little white dresses to put on for operating and underneath that we had scarcely any underwear—no bras, they were worn out and no one thought to send us clothes. And Madame came in a beautiful fur coat and fur-lined knee boots. I ought to have guessed she was Russian. She was very handsome in a hard way, but I'll never forget we were expected to line up for inspection which was something we never did, were not used to—so, we didn't.[27]

Lillian's rebel gene came bounding to the fore when 'Madame' ordered that the whole medical team line up before her. Incredulous that they were all expected to stop work and line up, Lillian pretended that she did not understand. '*Camarada, disciplina,* an order is an order,' hissed one of the Spanish orderlies. Lillian recalls her reply:

Irene was with me, and she had been a nurse on the New York waterfront working for the Communist Party during their brawls. Irene could swear very fluently in longshoreman language. I picked up the expression "Sod it!" So, I said the equivalent of "Sod it!" and left it at that.

But Lillian did not leave it at that, as she herself later confesses:

The next thing, I got a whiff of *eau de cologne* which made me mad as hell because we were filthy. Water was always off when you got bombed. You had no soap, the patients had it first. And there was always this feeling that you felt dirty and certainly at a disadvantage with a woman who was immaculate. [...] She came walking round and she started criticizing and in my presence she criticized dirt on the floor so I said, in Spanish, "As you're not a nurse, perhaps you wouldn't mind helping to clean the floor? We don't have enough people for cleaning." So, I didn't hit it off with her, after that and kept out of her way.[28]

Thankfully, adds Lillian, it was not long before 'Madame' packed up and left.

Another famous visitor with whom Lillian came into contact was Ernest Hemingway.[29] She recalls that he was keen to write a report on the nurses who had volunteered with the American Medical Bureau but found himself in a quandary when his secretary succumbed to dysentery. Lillian takes up the story:

So, whilst I was looking after the secretary for 48 hours, Hemingway was absolutely lost without a secretary. Big, brash Hemingway couldn't type, or if he could he wasn't going to admit it. I had read Hemingway, especially *Farewell to Arms*, like most people, so I said, 'I can type.' I don't know why I said it because I couldn't. So, he gave me a sheaf of notes and he said: 'How long will it take you to type these?' So, I said, 'Leave me alone and give me some paper.' He asked if I wanted any carbon. I was very dumb, but I realized that was something I needed. A Spanish orderly came and showed me how to use the typewriter. So, two fingers and I typed out some of his reports and I carried a carbon copy around with me for years.[30]

It will be remembered that while awaiting orders to move, between offensives, Lillian and Dorothy went to the assistance of an American équipe. When they eventually returned to their unit, they were given a far from warm welcome. Their colleagues refused even to speak to them.

When we got there we found that we were rather in disgrace as we'd gone off and taken part in action without anyone's permission [...] One of my protégées, Aurora, just wouldn't talk to me at all. All she could say was that we had disobeyed orders. But we hadn't had any orders! There was no doctor with us at the time and we had obeyed our instincts [...] And there was an aura about the room that we were in great disgrace somehow and that no one wanted us as we'd done something unspeakable.[31]

The tension was increased by the presence of an official-looking visitor, a political commissar come to discover more about their grave misdemeanour. The two women were grateful for the arrival of Dr Len Crome.[32] 'He was a wonderful doctor,' said Lillian, 'humane, and looking at Dorothy and me—we were filthy and dirty and tired out and hungry and thirsty and lousy and he just knew that we had been through the mill.' Crome approached the women, patted Lillian on the back, and asked her if she wanted to work with the Spaniards. 'Well, doctor,' she replied, 'that's what we're here for.' When the commissar asked for details of the reported trouble, Crome's response was swift: 'There isn't any trouble here,' he declared. Then, turning towards the two bedraggled, bug-bitten women he continued: 'Now, go and get some food and have a good night's sleep.'

Chapter Seven:
Medical provision for the battle of Teruel

The next major battle, Teruel, began at the end of December. Teruel registers the lowest winter temperatures in Spain, and 1937 was a particularly bad winter, making conditions extremely difficult. Temperatures ranged from six to twenty degrees below zero, at an altitude of some 1,200 metres and often in strong winds. Troops had to spend long periods in biting cold, rain and snow which led to exposure and frostbite and, in many cases, to the amputation of limbs. Lillian describes her experience of Teruel:

> Snow was many feet deep. Many of the men did not possess gloves or waterproof shoes. The cases I saw were chiefly frost-bitten toes, and only one or two with frost-bitten hands. After massage had been given, without success, we wrapped up the parts well in cotton wool, gave copious hot fluids to drink, and applied many blankets, the weight of these being kept off the patient's feet by inserting a box under the bedclothes or improvising cradles out of Kramer wire. These did not receive further treatment with us but were sent further down the lines.[1]

In total, the number of wounded and infirm Republican soldiers was around 60,000, a third of these due to frostbite.[2] In particular danger were those men on night guard duty, who had to remain motionless for several hours in the open in front-line positions and, thus, without the possibility of igniting fires. Officials of both armies took measures to reduce the risks of exposure by shortening the duration of night watches and by ensuring, as far as was possible, the correct clothing of troops.

Several of the hospitals set up in Teruel had British

medical staff. Dr Doug Jolly was operating with the 45th Division. Nurse Kathleen Cresswell and two British drivers, Charlie Innocent and Jim Smythe were at a small front-line hospital with the American, Dr Furhman, and the Spanish surgeon, Quemada. With the 35th Division at Cuevas Labradas were doctors Saxton and Kiszley, the medical student, Gerald Shirlaw, (Jerry Steele) and the American, William Pike, who assisted Len Crome in his administration of the 35th Division Medical Service. The team of nurses with Lillian included British nurse, Joan Purser, South African, Ada Hodson and Australian, Una Wilson. Englishman Keith (Andy) Andrews and American, Robert Webster were responsible for the sterilisation of surgical instruments while Percy Cohen drove the Rolls Royce ambulance donated by Lord Faringdon.[3]

Harry Evans, Chris Thornycroft and Max Colin were in charge of the transport park at Perales del Alfambra, north of Teruel. It was their job to maintain the lorries and ambulances and keep them on the road, a very difficult task under the extreme climatic conditions. During the battle of Teruel, the wounded were evacuated to Benicassim, which later became a convalescent centre for International Brigaders, and to Murcia and Valadaroz where there were hospitals specialising in particular kinds of care such as radiotherapy and physiotherapy. Aurora Fernández, one of the Spanish *chicas* with whom Lillian worked, describes their arrival at Cuevas Labradas for the battle of Teruel.

> After much travelling and many hairpin bends and snowbound roads sometimes blocked for days our lorries and trucks got to a small mountain village. Trembling with cold we turned an old watermill into our hospital. The Teruel attack had begun.[4]

'There was no town', remembers Lillian, 'It was just a place where very poor Spanish families have lived for generations, ... and gypsies.' They were so near the front line that severe wounds could be treated within an hour. As well as the British doctors, there were now three surgeons, American, Dr Barsky, Belgian, Dr Dumont and Catalan, Dr Broggi, who each led an *équipe*. They were also joined by British nurses Phyllis Hibbert and Dorothy Rutter, and Americans Esther Silverstein and Irene Goldin.

Teruel had been taken by the insurgents at the beginning of the war. By the end of 1937 it was almost surrounded by Republican troops. Their attack on Teruel was an attempt to prevent the rebels launching a major assault on Madrid through Guadalajara. The battle of Teruel, fought between 15 December 1937 and 22 February 1938, was arguably the toughest battle of the war—it was certainly fought in the harshest conditions. Here, it became clear that the Popular Army had progressed as a fighting force. However, it was also here that it lost some of its best units in weeks of bitter struggle that ultimately ended in defeat. Winifred Bates writes from Teruel:

> I am with the medical services and we are nearer the front than any hospital has ever been. Ankle-deep in mud, surrounded by ruined houses, living always within the sound of booming artillery, we are faced hour after hour, day after day with grim reality. All is well organised. Surgeons are specialising on cases, abdominal wounds being treated in the first hospitals, limbs a little further on, a hospital for sickness and frostbite in another place. Mobile équipes [...] move from place to place, rapidly and efficiently setting up operating rooms wherever they are wanted. Ambulances run to and fro, bring in men from the line, and evacuate them to the rear after operation. Stretcher-bearers go in and out.[5]

The *autochir* donated by the Society of Lithographic Artists and Designers in England was driven to Teruel just before Christmas by Charles Innocent and Jim Smyth. In the knowledge that they were carrying vital medical supplies badly needed at the front, they battled through terrible conditions to get to the hospital before the mountain roads were closed by blizzards. Dr Reginald Saxton was in charge of blood transfusion. Preserved blood was being supplied from the institutes established in Valencia and Barcelona, but the lack of a refrigerator meant that it was impossible to store it in any quantity and Saxton had to rely on donors from among the medical personnel, including Lillian.

Somewhat isolated and with no radio or newspapers the medical team gauged how the battle was going by the number of wounded they were receiving.

Spirits were high when the republican army took Teruel—the first provincial capital to fall into Republican hands. 'We were feeling pretty jubilant', recalls Lillian, 'but the casualties were pretty grim because all the way up to Teruel was snowbound, hard and rocky, so no one could dig trenches deep enough.' This meant that in addition to the usual head and chest wounds, there were a variety of other serious injuries to deal with, as Lillian explains:

> There were abdominal wounds galore and also what was very sad, wounds in the groin and that was one kind of injury that the Spaniard just couldn't take. His manhood was taken away and when you had to break the news gently to them when they were out of the anaesthetic, they would fumble around with their bandages and find something was wrong and they had a tube in their bladder, or what was left of their bladder, there would be a ghastly shout '*Ya no soy hombre!*' (I'm not a man any more!) I had to go and sedate them and talk to them about the wonders of sulphur drugs, which were fairly miraculous in those days. We had to stay with them and hope they wouldn't be tempted to commit suicide.[6]

Despite the extreme conditions in which they lived and worked, Lillian often found herself inspired by her colleagues. There was a true spirit of cooperation and support, and the hospitals were run largely on a democratic basis. There was often open discussion as to how best to deal with the medical situations encountered, recalls Lillian. 'We would talk in groups, and someone would say, 'Should I take over the theatre?' or 'Should I do anaesthetics?' […] 'Shall I take over *triaje*?' And there was never any long-winded discussion. It was always known that someone was going to take over and it was always the person best suited for the job.'[7]

Aurora Fernández also notes that the hospital functioned very well, but with one major impediment—lice. At times it was impossible for the medical staff to wash either themselves or their patients for lack of soap, and sometimes of water, and little could be done to prevent the frequent infestations of lice and fleas that plagued staff and patients alike, especially during the summer months. Now, when washing was almost impossible due to the freezing weather, explains Fernández, 'we scratched and scratched day and night'. The itching was so bad that, at times, she found it impossible to sleep and resorted to a drastic and somewhat dangerous practice. 'I had the idea to pinch a little ether for anaesthetics and pour a little on, so the lice slept and also myself […] it was an English nurse called Lillian Urmston, who was very efficient and good, who told me not to do that. "Everyone is smoking here", she warned, "and you could go up in flames".'[8]

Determined to retake the city, Franco cancelled his attack on Madrid and concentrated his forces in Teruel. The fierce counter-offensive began in mid-January. The unrelenting air attacks grew ever fiercer. Winifred Bates describes conditions for the medical personnel who had to work under aerial bombardment and to the sound of incessant artillery:

As soon as the clouds break the fascist aeroplanes rise in groups of thirty or more, and, skimming the hill-tops, they make towards the village. The civilian population has already trooped out to hide in holes in the hills. Against the clear blue sky we watch the black bombers move in formation […] over the place where we assume the trenches to be. And our minds sicken as the peppering of machine-gun fire is heard. The ambulances are not coming in. They are waiting till dark and we know what the night will bring. Sometimes the aeroplanes do not turn back but come straight towards us. Yesterday they came from four directions and made the swastika pattern above the hospital. Then they broke formation and swooped. They machine-gunned the walls and the roof and the blankets lying out in the sun. They flung incendiary bombs all round [...] For six hours the attack on the village and the hospital went on. We had no food all day, for the cooks work and we eat, outside in a lean-to shed in the yard. We did what we could for the wounded.[9]

Events spurred on those in Britain campaigning to end the government's adherence to the Treaty of Non-Intervention. Had the policy been applied equally to both sides in the conflict, it might have been seen as acceptable, but the arms embargo was completely one-sided 'which makes one question the integrity as well as the logic of the men proclaiming neutrality', declared political activist, Emma Goldman:

It is not only the height of folly, it is also the height of inhumanity to sacrifice the larger part of the Spanish people to a small minority of Spanish adventurers armed with every modern device of war [...] Is it possible that the liberal world outside Spain will stand by and see the country laid in ashes by the Fascist hordes? Or will they muster up enough courage to break through the bars of neutrality and come to the rescue of the Spanish people?[10]

Even Lillian herself, who professed to be completely apolitical, had something to say on the matter of non-intervention. She wrote to the SMAC in London:

why is it that the workers of England [...] have still not

united themselves into a body strong enough to break down the farcical 'Non-Intervention'? We are all grateful for anything that is sent to Spain, but why cannot we have all the arms we need? I guess I could rave like this for ever, I'm so ashamed of the British Government. [11]

Despite the fervor of such convictions and the eloquence of the arguments, all attempts to persuade the British Government as to the utter injustice of non-intervention proved futile.

In February, the Republicans suffered a spectacular defeat on the Alfambra River, to the northeast of the city of Teruel and thousands of soldiers died or were taken prisoner. On 22 February, with rebel victory imminent, the Republicans evacuated the city, both sides having suffered many thousands of losses. When the retreats from Teruel began, the medical team was faced with a rapid influx of casualties. 'The Teruel retreat was hell. It was hell,' affirms Lillian. At one point, the team comprised only two doctors—both Spanish and only one of them fully qualified, three Spanish *chicas*, and several orderlies. However, the orderlies were tremendously useful. 'There were some orderlies who were just born to be medics,' recalls Lillian, and they could be relied upon in times of emergency.

> I could say, 'Right, I've got into this man's vein, his group is such and such, send to the fridge for number 1 blood, and I'd write on his hand what it was. And then for another man we got drips out and I'd write on his hand again, and then it was foolproof. That was the only way to do it, there was no time to write instructions. There was no time to write report books and had there been we didn't have the paper or pens and ink.[12]

Not all the assistants were so steadfast. One of the drivers, Butt, a Canadian Communist, was reliable, recalls Lillian, as long as he had not had access to alcohol. Preventing this was crucial at the time, as the team had only two ambulances and the drivers were running flat out in a shuttle service, with one ambulance always at the front line and one in reserve. This, in itself, brought particular danger. 'Fighting rearguard action was what I called leapfrogging', explains Lillian. 'You'd leap backwards then someone else would let you retreat, then they themselves would leap backwards and others would take over, and so on. And we got lots of fractures that way because there were no lights at all, ambulances drove in sheer darkness.'[13]

When the nurses heard a vehicle arriving at the hospital, especially if there was more than one, they were often terror-stricken, not at the thought of the loads of casualties they might bring, if, indeed, they were ambulances, but the uncertainty as to whether or not they might be the enemy. They had all heard of the atrocities being committed by the insurgents' Moorish troops in the areas they had taken and patients and hospital staff were not exempted. For example, Werner Heilbrun, a doctor with the XII International Brigade, observed from a hilltop as the battle of Jarama drew to a close. Later he described the devastating scene:

> The wounded were lined up in stretchers along the Chinchón road. I wanted to go to them but they persuaded me against it. When all the troops were beaten, one-by-one the Moors killed all the wounded on stretchers. I asked myself how one can go on living after seeing that.[14]

Rape and other forms of gender violence were common tactics of the Nationalist forces and their allies during the Civil War. Moroccan *regulares* were ordered to rape women to provoke terror among local populaces.[15] Lillian Urmston describes the effect that this had on the nursing team:

> There was that horrible feeling—'my God!'—rapes galore [...] I'm afraid we all worried about that and that was when people started to talk about things like venereal disease,

that it would be worse to have that. And so, whenever we heard these things we had that awful feeling that we ought to damn well hide or get under the patients' beds. But if the Moors were there they often went into wards and killed the patients. So, we knew damn well that if the worst came to the worst, to hide anywhere near a patient would be disaster. And we literally used to look after each other afterwards and someone would say to me: 'Lillian, what happened to your knees?' Because after the crisis was over, and it turned out to be our trucks, our ambulances, my knees would knock for hours on end. The other girls would go deathly white and vomit.[16]

The republicans did their best to hold up the retreat, but after three days defence collapsed and chaos ensued. By the last week in February, Teruel was in fascist hands. Those republican troops who survived Teruel were exhausted and demoralised, and a great deal of matériel, especially aircraft and artillery, was lost. In the following weeks, Franco took full advantage of the situation by launching an all-out attack on Aragon that would open the rebels' passage to the Mediterranean. Lillian and her équipe had orders to evacuate all patients from the hospital. This was carried out successfully before the staff received their own orders to move. Winifred Bates describes the event.

Lilian [sic] Urmston and I went to bed at 1 am. At 4.30 the other nurses awakened us. Lilian, Dorothy Rutter and two of the American nurses had orders to move at once to another place. So they packed up their équipe and went. Later I followed them and saw with what skill they went into any building that might be allotted to them and set up an operating theatre and a ward. It took them less than half a day. I saw them work for 24 and 36 hours at a stretch.[17]

Then followed a period of waiting. The one constant feature of life in the hospital in which Lillian now found herself was the incessant rain—so much so that the nearby river rose steadily until it reached the door of the hospital, which was only a wooden hut. Orders were issued to pack up and move, but this was impossible as the floods prevented any lorries from approaching the hospital for two or three weeks. Food supplies were very low and of very poor quality. 'We each keep a bit of quite moldy bread under the pillow to nibble at night,' wrote Rosaleen Smythe, SMAC Secretary and personnel officer, 'Oh, for something to put on it.'

> We are allowed a small piece of cheese and a small piece of sausage. There is tense excitement when trading sausage for cheese begins. We have to go half a mile to the kitchen for food in the mud and the dark. As we are expecting to move, we have discharged the civil personnel. I have been doing the kitchen work with the two American nurses, Esther and Irene. [...] We can hear the guns all day. We have half a tank of drinking water left. The lorries have not yet got through the mud. The wards are filling with influenza cases [...] Dr Saxton has to chlorinate the water every morning. There is absolutely no sanitation of any kind. The cases are increasing. We have no clean water, no fires, no heating, no lavatories.[18]

All this, adds Smythe, together with the incessant rain and the rats, made existence a misery. Nevertheless, she adds: 'I cannot say enough about the splendid way Ada Hodson, Patience Darton and Lilian [sic] Urmston are working. [...] Lilian's morale is never destroyed; I admire her.'

Lillian did, indeed, display a more positive, resilient attitude. She declared that in spite of the extremely uncomfortable circumstances morale was high. It was only the frequent bombing raids to which they were subject that occasionally caused panic. She remembers one in particular. Those patients who were able ran outside and took cover in the creeks of the river. The rest could only lie and wait. Lillian was on night duty at the time and was in bed. She takes up the story:

> It's a good job that in these emergencies one's mind functions, even though one's body feels petrified. Lola, a young Spanish girl, had been sitting on my bed trying very hard to learn the English alphabet. She was much too afraid to dash outside for cover. So, my first move was to push her under my bed. I felt almost too afraid to move but went into the ward to talk to the men [...] Then for what seemed endless minutes a succession of bombs fell. During these minutes I felt very aloof, and nothing seemed to matter. I talked to the men, but do not know of what I talked. All the time I was listening for the shrieking of a bomb which I felt sure must fall on our hospital. One fell just outside, and two huge pieces of wood crashed down from the roof. We tried, and I think managed to joke about it. As the bombs fell near, we all threw ourselves down on the floor. I shall never forget Lola's face so scared, peering at me from under the bed and she still had a piece of chocolate, which we had been about to eat, clutched in her hand.[19]

In the confusion after the retreats from Teruel, the medical personnel became dispersed, and Lillian found herself 'more and more attached to the Spaniards.'[20] She ended up with a Spanish team at Ulldemolins, in what was then a hospital of the XV Army Corps. She was visited there by Leah Manning at the head of a small British delegation undertaking a tour of International Brigade hospitals. Manning described the hospital as 'quite a small 30-bed hospital established in a modern school building'.[21] She adds that Lillian Urmston was there, with Dr Olsina for nearly six months.[22] Again, we can only read between the lines of Manning's report:

> she is the nurse who left Fraga with Patience Darton after the row with Aquilo [sic], and whom we recalled but who

would not come back. After a conversation with her, I think there was perhaps something to be said on both sides. [23]

Mindful of Lillian's feisty, independent character and sense of justice, it should probably not surprise us that she (together with Patience) had walked out on the Spanish surgeon after an argument. Furthermore, Manning implies that there was a good reason for her actions:

> she is doing extremely good work now and although she has been shut away in this tiny village high up in the mountains there was every evidence that the peasants in that village regarded her with the very deepest affection. When we arrived, the hospital had been evacuated and Lillian was waiting for the orders for her équipe to move up to the front. Working with her is an exceptionally intelligent *chica* named Lola [...] In the big retreat this girl was nearly caught by the Fascists but managed with incredible courage to escape across two rivers and over two mountain ranges down to Valls. When the orders to move came, she moved with Lillian and we saw her up at the front that night. [24]

Chapter Eight:
Medical provision for the battle of the Ebro

The battle of Teruel had proven costly in terms of men and military matériel. When the Nationalists then immediately launched an offensive in Aragon, in March, the exhausted Republican army could offer little resistance. However, on 17 March 1938, after the Anschluss, the French frontier was reopened, and the Republican Army in Catalonia received 18,000 tons of war matériel.[1] The Republic extended the age-range of conscription to include middle-aged men and youths from as young as sixteen years old, the latter forming the so-called *Quinta del Biberón* (the Baby-bottle Regiment). These new recruits would help to form the Army of the Ebro.[2]

Franco now moved his troops towards Valencia with the aim of taking Madrid and the central front. In an attempt to relieve the pressure on Valencia and Madrid and to recover Catalan territory, Negrín ordered an attack across the fast-flowing river Ebro. Communist General Juan Modesto was in charge of the offensive of which the initial objective was to recapture the strategic Nationalist stronghold of Gandesa (about twenty-five kilometres west of the river).

The battle of the Ebro, widely recognized as the longest and bloodiest battle of the Spanish Civil War, was the last battle in which the medical units of the International Brigades would be involved. In preparation for the offensive, there was some reorganisation of the medical services. The *équipe* that had been with the 35th Division became the medical unit of the XV Army Corps, with Dr Leonard Crome as Chief Medical Officer.

From the beginning of July, the Republican troops had undergone increasingly more intensive training and when this began to include a simulated river-crossing, it became obvious that there was to be an offensive across the Ebro.

Within a quarter of a mile of the river, the narrow country lanes became packed with troops and vehicles carrying rowing boats, pontoons, and other such equipment. Over 80,000 Republican troops, including the 15th International Brigade and the British Battalion, began crossing the river on 25 July, establishing a bridgehead on the west bank and advancing towards the town of Gandesa. The element of surprise appeared to be effective, and the initial advance was rapid, with the Republican forces gaining territory and capturing prisoners. However, the Francoists held strongly fortified positions in the hills around Gandesa and long and bitter battles ensued, causing an enormous number of republican casualties. The medical teams would be working day and night for the duration of the battle.

The *Sanidad Militar* of the Army of the Ebro ordered the creation of front-line hospitals in accordance with standard practice. They should be near enough to the battle lines to be able to perform life-saving surgery within the shortest time possible, but not so exposed to enemy fire as to jeopardise the safety of the patients. The other chief requisite was the existence of an adequate system of evacuation—usually by road or rail. Emergency field hospitals for the battle of the Ebro would be installed in hermitages, caves, and railway tunnels. One of the most important facilities was the Santa Lucía cave hospital at La Bisbal de Falset, which provided hospital support for the Flix and Ascó sectors. There were also three hospital trains: Number 20 was stationed inside the tunnel in Argentera, at the Pradell de la Teixeta station and trains Number 12 and Number 5 were in the tunnel of Guiamets station. When the wounded had been treated, they would be transferred by hospital trains to the Evacuation Hospital of the Army of the Ebro within the complex of the psychiatric sanatorium Pere Mata de Reus. The V Army Corps wounded were sent to the field hospitals located in Perelló, l'Ampolla and l'Ametlla de Mar, near the Barcelona-Valencia railway line. From here they were evacuated to the Army Base

Hospital in Cambrils and from there by train to the Base Hospital of the Army of the Ebro at Sabinosa in Tarragona.[3]

Leah Manning was inspecting the medical facilities in which British volunteers were preparing for the battle of the Ebro. She and her companions set out for the cave in Tarragona that the British had converted into a hospital. Known locally as the "cova hospital de Santa Llúcia" (Santa Lucía cave hospital) it lay in the mountains about a kilometre from the town of La Bisbal de Falset. As they went higher and higher into the mountains, the visitors got lost and had to stop and ask for directions. Even after assistance from the local inhabitants, declared Manning, 'we had to keep our eyes well skinned, or we never would have discovered it.' She describes the scene when they finally arrived:

> Down in a great hollow between an encircling wall of mountains with trees affording a safe cover stood Reggie Saxton's blood transfusion van, three *autochirs*, Ada Hodson's marquee and a smaller marquee where the Jefatura has its office. Here Nan Green as secretary was busily typing away. Much *impedimenta* but not a sign of a hospital. To this we had to be led by circuitous paths (very hard on me, halfway up the mountain) on the opposite side to which we had come down, to an enormous natural cave in the mountain side, which had been cleverly blasted to make a great ward for sixty beds, a triage, an operating theatre and a kitchen. I suppose that in all the history of modern warfare there has never been such a hospital. It is the safest place in Spain, beautifully wired for electric lights and with every kind of modern equipment. This hospital is evacuated twice a day. It is tragic to add that a large proportion of the evacuations are by death, because only the gravest cases are brought here from the front, and the only ones who remain for longer than the first day or two are abdominals and serious amputations.[4]

There is some discrepancy in the estimations of the number of beds offered by the cave hospital. The most reliable estimate is probably that made by Doug Jolly, head surgeon with one of the six surgical teams working in the cave. He puts the figure at 150.[5] Each day, the bodies of the deceased were taken by lorry to the local cemetery, just outside the village, where they were buried in communal graves dug along the cemetery's boundary walls.[6]

Patience Darton and Ada Hodson were on duty when Manning arrived at the cave hospital. As she went into the cave, a soldier from the British Battalion was stretchered in. He was gravely wounded in the abdomen. He had his spleen removed and Reg Saxton gave him a blood transfusion. 'As I stood by he opened his eyes and spoke my name', recounts Manning:

> I recognised him as a comrade whom I had met at a bye-election in South Wales, a miner from Tonypandy named Harry Dobson. Dr Jolly told me that it was not possible that he could live, in fact they thought only a few hours, so I determined to stay by him until the end. Actually, it was fifteen hours before he passed away but I did not leave him during that time and he seemed very happy to have me there.[7]

Saxton gave Dobson a further blood transfusion, for which Winifred Bates' blood was used. The medical team did everything possible for him, but there was no hope. All that there remained to do was to ease his pain and to accompany him as he drifted into unconsciousness. There were several other extremely grave cases needing similar intensive care and the medical staff worked ceaselessly through the night. Manning continues:

> It was a fantastic night, as I sat by this dying comrade, passing along the high winding road on the side opposite from the cave, hundreds of camions passed by with singing reserves and loads of material and ammunition on their way to the Ebro, whilst winding down to the path to the

glen at the bottom, came the ambulances with dead, dying and wounded men.[8]

The next morning, Manning's small team set out to visit the evacuation train where nurses Ann Murray and Margaret de Culpeper were working with Spanish doctors Quemada and D'Harcourt. As they were about to leave, Charlie Innocent pulled up in an ambulance full of wounded from the Ebro, and Lillian Urmston arrived from Ulldemolins. Lillian had received orders to move, in preparation for the battle of the Ebro. She tells her part of the story in the lead up to the battle:

> We were all keyed-up with excitement. July—just three months after our ghastly retreat—and we were prepared for an offensive, which, even if only partially successful, could hold up the Fascist drive on the southern front and also show the whole world what Republican Spain can achieve [...] We took a huge cave—our first bomb-proof hospital and installed 120 beds. The narrow end of the cave was 'sheeted off' to serve as offices, operating room, etc. In the valley below was a small colony of tents— dressing, classification and evacuation posts.[9]

Over the next few days ambulances came and went day and night, and the wounded poured in in a constant stream. (There were civilian patients as well as soldiers.) Throughout the day, the Nationalists bombed the pontoon bridges and throughout the night republican work battalions repaired them. It was an arduous and very dangerous task to get the wounded back across the river to the cave hospital at La Bisbal de Falset, so only the worst cases were brought in. They were brought across the river on the pontoon bridges or rowed across, at night, on the boats of local peasants, after having been hidden until nightfall along the riverbank. The mortality rate for the hospital was, therefore, understandably high. All this, together with a scarcity of food, made conditions almost unbearable. The members of staff who worked there recall the mouldy bread, the donkey meat, and the very great suffering they were obliged to witness. Winifred Bates writes:

> Men died as I stood beside them. It was summer time and they had been in long training before they crossed the Ebro. Their bodies were brown and beautiful [...] It is so hard to make a man, and so easy to blast him to death. I shall never forget the Ebro. If one went for a walk away from the cave there was the smell of death.[10]

Word soon got round that hundreds of wounded men were lying on the other side of the river and could not be brought across. 'We were all sick with horror at the thought of this unnecessary suffering and begged our chiefs to send us across the river,' declared Lillian. She remembered clearly when, on 29 July, three of the six teams operating in the cave hospital received orders to move:

> at 1 a.m., the Spanish Medical Director told me to pack equipment and be ready in 20 minutes to move across the river. I hurriedly issued orders, and in a very short time we were ready. I was to go along with Dr Jolly, the Spanish doctors and *sanitarios* (medical auxiliaries) and set up as large a hospital as possible.[11]

Theirs was one of the first medical units to cross the Ebro. 'The difficulties that had to be overcome even to reach the river were too numerous to describe,' recalls Lillian. Then, crossing the river on the pontoon bridge, the ambulance broke down and had to be towed the rest of the way by a truck. They reached the other side just as dawn was breaking, and to the familiar cry of *aviación*! The ambulances were pulled up at the side of the road, under the shelter of the cliffs. Lillian continues:

we lay in ditches, tense with expectation and apprehension. But it was only our usual early morning caller, the observation plane. We continued our journey for exactly 25 minutes, and then twelve huge bombers came into sight. We all pulled into an olive grove, just off the road, and hastily camouflaged our ambulances and autochir. Then, a brief whistle—no movement—and we all lay down under trees and bushes. The planes bombed all along the riverbanks, and roads and crossroads.

A written account that Lillian gave at the time was published in the monthly SMAC bulletin. The exhilarating, almost sensationalist tone would surely be considered offensive today. However, we should bear in mind the propagandist nature of the piece and judge it against the standards of acceptability of the day:

Suddenly came the familiar rat-tat-tat of machine guns—they were strafing the helpless people who happened to be anywhere in view. At last came a number, six I think, of our pursuit planes, and engaged in a glorious dog fight. It is a most stimulating sight, this, to see our small planes tackling these gigantic bombers. After an hour of this the bombers soared higher and disappeared. We were all relieved. And weren't we hungry! Rations of bully beef and bread were issued, then we again moved off. At 2 p.m. we reached Santa Magdalena, a huge white hermitage set high on the hills. Rather a landmark—but the only available habitation. We cheerfully acted as charwomen, then quickly set up a hospital. We were again interrupted by a heavy bombardment—luckily the bombs did not fall too near. By 11 p.m. our hospital was complete, and a steady stream of ambulances started to arrive. We only received the more severely wounded cases and our beds were quickly filled.[12]

Mas de Santa Magdalena Hospital

The Mas de Santa Magdalena Hospital was created on 29 July 1938, under the orders of Dr Len Crome. Three surgical teams (with autochirs) were redeployed from the cave hospital at La Bisbal de Falset and advanced with a section of the Army Corps to the bank of the river Ebro at Ascó, where a bridge was being constructed. The three teams crossed the completed bridge at dawn, with the objective of establishing a hospital in the Chapel of Santa Magdalena, at a road junction in the mountains near Camposines, from where they would evacuate their wounded to Ascó or Móra d'Ebre. Although it was in a somewhat exposed position, six surgical teams would work here for the following three months.[13] Catalan surgeon, Miquel Gras i Artero, led one of the teams. On 29 July 1938, he received an order from the head of the Campaign Hospital of the XV Army Corps ordering him to move with his team from the cave hospital in La Bisbal de Falset to the town of Móra la Nova, where he crossed the river to Móra d'Ebre.[14] He worked there, briefly, in a small campaign hospital in anti-aircraft shelters before going on to the hospital in the Mas de Santa Magdalena.[15]

The installation of the new hospital was complete by 11.00 pm, and the wounded poured in as soon as it was operational. As Lillian notes, it was soon full. The medical team worked in challenging conditions, not least because there were enemy planes overhead throughout the day, bombing bridges and roads and other infrastructure. Lillian reports for the SMAC:

All day long we had the enemy planes overhead. Bridge and roads were bombed daily, and many ambulances were smashed and rendered unfit for use. Work continued but under great difficulties. Food and medical supplies could not be regularly brought across the river—so belts were tightened and brains were racked to provide a solution to the problem of medical supplies. Many and varied were the ideas produced. One day about 9 am we were again 'disturbed' by the whistle of shells overhead—the fascists had centred on us their heavy guns.[16]

The Mas de Santa Magdalena hospital formed part of the medical services of the 35th division, which was the unit engaged in the advance on Gandesa. Fighting was intense and casualties were many and its nearness to the front-line meant that Santa Magdalena played a role of crucial importance on the Ebro Front. There were up to six surgical teams working there, with their respective *autochirs* stationed in the nearby olive grove. One équipe was led by Commander Douglas Jolly and another was headed by Captain Miquel Gras i Artero but we also know that from 22 of August 1938 Dr Ruiz i Curto was transferred to the hospital.[17] When Francoist forces occupied the Sierra de Cavalls, bringing the frontline dangerously close to the hospital, it was obliged to uproot once more, in search of a safer site.

Flix railway tunnel hospital: civilian patients

The site decided upon was a large railway tunnel at Flix, about 10 kilometres away, on the edge of the river Ebro. After another anxious night drive without lights, the team reached the new site as dawn was breaking. Before the hospital could be set up, they had to remove, as best they could, the soot and grime enveloping the walls and ceiling. Lillian describes the scene:

> We stumbled along in the dark, continually falling over railway lines. Everyone was cold, tired and hungry—but the hospital had to be prepared. We all worked furiously, digging, scraping and scrubbing and soon we had ready another hospital complete with 65 beds. But oh! Wouldn't a coat of whitewash work wonders.[18]

There was a poor electricity supply and inadequate lighting, with one lamp powered by a small generator, for three operating tables. Other work had to be carried out by candlelight. However, even this did not last long. After two days, the reserves of candles and oil ran out and the nursing staff resorted to giving injections and carrying out other procedures by the light of matches. Instruments were sterilized in fish kettles on primus stoves and the only warmth for the patients was that generated by burning alcohol in open pans, a dangerous practice as ether was being used for anaesthetics. In typical fashion, Lillian's spirits remained undampened.

> By degrees, many minor luxuries were installed in our tunnel although bombings were frequent! Occasionally a bomb fell directly above us and then we were all enveloped in soot. Rather bad luck if one had just shampooed one's hair in the river Ebro![19]

In the area around the Flix tunnel, Lillian recalls obvious signs of wealth, with 'lovely villas and farmhouses', indicating that it had once been Nationalist territory:

> we were able to ransack those places and find linen for the beds and so on. We set up a theatre under beautiful linen sheets and made a canopy in the tunnel and a sort of post-op recovery room. We had all that laid out under beautiful linen sheets—some of them bearing crests.[20]

Throughout the war, British (and other) medical personnel often found themselves treating civilians and even wounded Nationalist troops, when the need arose. Whenever emergency hospitals were set up, they would be visited by local people in need of treatment. 'Needless to say,' affirms Lillian, 'they were never turned away.' The medical volunteers dealt with all who attended their clinics—from pregnant women and newborn infants to senior citizens. In base hospitals and convalescent centres, away from the front lines, this was taken into consideration in the organisation of the hospital, and special days were set aside, when possible, for the treatment of villagers. The SMAC Committee in London sent out the medical supplies necessary for this kind of work, the benefits of which were quite significant, as Lillian explains:

> Sometimes a doctor or a nurse would go out to a house in the village and attend to a maternity case. In some of the small outlying villages a midwife was unheard of. Thanks to our clinics, many early cases of tuberculosis, etc, were detected, and were thus able to receive the necessary treatment.[21]

Lillian goes on to give a touching testimony to this policy in her account of the time spent in the tunnel hospital at Flix in the summer of 1938:

> One afternoon we noticed a number of enemy aeroplanes passing overhead, and within a few minutes we could hear the terrific bombardment of a nearby village. We hastily ordered an evacuation of those of the wounded it was possible to move, for we knew from long experience that soon we would have numbers of civilians brought to us. Among the first to be received was a young woman, eight and a half months pregnant. She had various head injuries (not very serious), a fracture of the lower end of the humerus, a superficial abdominal wound, and a nasty gash in the thigh. All the usual symptoms of shock were present, and we could not feel the radial pulse beat.

She was covered with a blanket and while the orderlies placed hot-water bottles around her Lillian administered 2cc of caffeine intravenously. By this time the woman's pulse was discernible, though still extremely weak and rapid, and her breathing became steady. As the severity of the shock lessened, the frightened woman protested to having an injection, and gazed at Lillian with obvious suspicion. Observing this, the Spanish doctor in charge instructed the orderly to give her morphia. Lillian continues:

> I stayed with her until the surgeon decided to take her into the theatre. The wounds were cleaned, edges excised, then sutured, and the arm put into an 'aeroplane' splint made of Kramer wire. She was then handed over to me. I kept her in a corner bed for greater seclusion and easier observation. When she recovered consciousness, I reassured her but explained that frequent injections were necessary. Her chief concern was for the baby. I told her that we were giving her all the treatment not merely for her sake but for that of the baby.[22]

The woman eventually came to trust Lillian—so much so that she would call her whenever she felt the need for medication or just a few words of comfort. Despite the distressful circumstances, Lillian recalls with precision the treatment she administered:

> This consisted of a 300cc intravenous injection of glucosade, followed by another one of saline four hours later. This was continued for 16 hours. Between these injections I gave her a cc of camphor in oil, when required. She also had one direct blood transfusion of 400cc. Afterwards I gave her an intramuscular injection of saline—300cc—every four or six hours.[23]

The medical team continued to work without respite as the bombing got closer. However, when it became evident that the entrance to the tunnel was the target for the bombs, with the consequent danger of entombing all those inside, the team was ordered to evacuate the patients and stand by to move. The above account of the case of the pregnant woman was one that Lillian gave in the professional nursing journal,

Nursing Mirror, shortly after the war. In a later interview, however, she gives a much more emotional, and understandably less clinically precise, version of events:

> The last operation I assisted was on a woman eight months pregnant with terrible chest and abdominal shrapnel wounds and a leg nearly blown off, and whilst we were attending to her, expecting to find the baby dead, she gave birth, despite those ghastly wounds, to a thriving little baby son. I gave her a blood transfusion afterwards. She was very proud of her little son, her *hijo*. She wanted to know my name and could she call him after me. I suggested Hugo or Jack Cade—again, the family name coming out. And she said, 'Hugo, Hugo!' So, it was decided, and we had to leave that poor woman in the tunnel. We could only evacuate military, we could not take civilians with us. We just hoped and prayed. I told her to say that she was Catholic and we found Catholic insignia [...] that I thought might have been useful to flog for a first aid kit somewhere, if I went through France, and I pinned it on this woman and I told her: 'You are a Catholic.' And I remember her smiling so proudly despite all those terrible injuries and she said: 'I was.' And I replied: 'You are again.' And I said: 'You'll be well taken care of. Keep this on you.' I kissed her and I kissed the baby, a lovely kid, and we just beat it.[24]

By this time, the long hours of stressful work in difficult conditions had taken their toll on Lillian's health. Suffering from bronchitis and both physically and psychologically exhausted, she decided to take leave. Although she made the request with some reluctance, she felt that she could raise substantial funding for medical aid if she could explain to people in England about the situation in Spain. Thus, it was that, at the end of September 1938, Lillian returned home to Stalybridge.

7. The British press report on Lillian's medical work in Spain.

8. Lilian entering the Santa Lucía cave hospital at La Bisbal de Falset, on the Ebro front, July 1938

9. Lillian with the Dutch commissar in the cave hospital.

10. The Dutch commissar enjoys a cigarette.

Chapter Nine:
From Stalybridge to the south of France: the *Retirada* and French concentration camps

Lillian's visit home was not entirely restful. The SMAC sent an ambulance out to her in Stalybridge and she toured the surrounding towns with it, talking to people about the situation in Spain. Keenly aware of the propaganda value of the exercise, Lillian instructed her SMAC colleagues to leave the ambulance exactly as it had been when it came back from Spain—shell-damaged and bloodstained.

> I spoke to Quakers, Church of England, Congregational, Methodist, Communist, Labour, Co-operative Women, Towns Women's Guild, you name it. And some of them were very skeptical about things even when they saw the ambulance [...] and my theme was that this is going to happen to us unless we put more into the Spanish War.[1]

Lillian tried to impress upon people the might of the aid that the insurgents were receiving from Nazi Germany and fascist Italy, and with which the Republic and the volunteers of the International Brigades were battling, against all odds. So successful was she in her endeavour that the people of Stalybridge started a 'Nurse Urmston Fund for Spanish Medical Aid'. This was followed by an invitation to breakfast from the local Catholic Priest. 'I was horrified at being invited out to breakfast and I thought it was something I'd better tell my mother about,' recalls Lillian. She and the priest had a good breakfast and retired to his study, where he proceeded to question her relentlessly for nearly two hours. He referred to the destruction of churches and other anti-religious atrocities allegedly being committed by the republicans, the gory 'details' of which were emblazoned all over the British press. Lillian did all she could to explain the reality of the situation, adding: 'We are entering churches that have been smashed during the fighting and we take them over as hospitals and until the fighting actually takes place in such an area there has not been all that desecration.' Concluding the meeting, the priest expressed his regret at being unable to contribute church coffers towards the cause, but wrote her a cheque for £25 out of his personal funds, requesting that the SMAC not be informed that the donation had been made by a Catholic priest. In all, some £700 was raised by house-to-house collection and public meetings—a remarkable amount for what was an economically distressed area.

By the first week in November, Lillian had spoken at over 30 meetings of various kinds. Some were political or religious events, while others were of a more general nature. They took place at an assortment of different venues, including private homes, schools, and church halls. She spoke from a Labour platform in Stalybridge, for example, but she was keen to point out the circumstances:

> my speech had no political significance. It was purely and simply in the interests of the wounded in Spain, to obtain medical supplies and food for them. I have said over and over again that I was prepared to speak from any political or religious platform to further this worthy cause. My work is purely humanitarian.[2]

Lillian received a great deal of support, not only in Stalybridge but in Hyde, Dunkinfield, Ashton, and even in Manchester and Kendal. In Hyde, the Women's Committee was extremely active. As well as making a small collection to donate to Spanish Medical Aid, the women knitted woollen garments to send out to the soldiers. Similar support was given in Ashton. However, Lillian was upset by a certain amount of negative reaction from some areas in Stalybridge, where there were complaints about sending money to Spain. 'If people here could only see the people there, there would be no question as to the need for any help, and they would give it,' asserted Lillian. 'I am going straight back to the front where I am required. If the worst comes and I do not return, well, I shall have done my duty. If I return, and my services are needed here, I feel I shall have gained some experience that will be useful.'[3]

She was given a rousing farewell party by some 80 friends and well-wishers, together with the local male voice choir, in the Congregational School, Stalybridge, and the following morning, many friends and members of the local appeal committee gave her a hearty send-off at Stalybridge Station. Shortly afterwards, the Reporter published a letter from Lillian herself, thanking the working-class people of Stalybridge who had contributed so generously to the house-to-house collections that had been made, and to those volunteers who had carried out the collections. She also paid tribute to the members of the Appeal for Spain Committee who had shown her unfailing support during her time in Stalybridge, concluding:

> I am going back to Spain because I feel it my duty to do so. This time, I am no longer ignorant of what war means. Now, I understand to the full—blockade, slow starvation of the population, continual bombardments and artillery fire, filth and disease. These things are just part of war. I am seeing children and babies growing up after two-and-a-half years of war, nervous wrecks, many of them with tuberculosis and rickets, devoid of nourishing food and warm clothes. Will you people of Stalybridge rally round the committee and, by your efforts, help alleviate the sufferings of a war-weary people?[4]

On Lillian's return to Spain, in early November, she was driven through France in a lorry by a SMAC volunteer. She did not learn a great deal about her driver, but one thing she remembered very clearly was that he seemed to know where all the very good restaurants were in various towns, 'and he never went into a simple little café,' she recalls, 'he had the money and I didn't query it, but the nearer I got to Spain the more it broke my heart to think of eating so well and the Spaniards waiting for anything I had.' Nevertheless, she was thrilled to be taking out substantial supplies.

> the people had at home had laden me up, even the local pharmacy and the manager of the Boots Chemist. I was known as 'Our Lillian'—they were rather proud of what 'Our Lillian' was achieving. They loaded me up with carbolic, soaps, bandages, disinfectants and they were not supposed to give me any drugs because I wasn't a doctor you see [...] but doctors used to leave parcels at my home and they were samples of drugs [...] and all this went back with me and I wouldn't let it out of my sight.[5]

On 21 September 1938, Spanish Prime Minister Juan Negrín had announced that the International Brigades were to be withdrawn. The decision had been made in the hope that, in consequence, the Non-Intervention Committee would put pressure on Franco to withdraw his German and Italian allies. Tragically, this did not come about, and many more men would lose their lives in the fighting on the Ebro, in a prolonged but intense battle of attrition.

In the Pandols and Cavalls mountains, the Republicans tried desperately to resist in the face of the rebels' far greater artillery power and superior troop numbers. The British Battalion would take part in one last fatal action in the Sierra de la Vall de la Torre, the mountain range between Corbera and Camposines. On 2 October, the Nationalists occupied the heights of La Vall and two weeks later Hill 666, the key point on the Sierra de Pandols.[6] On 30 October, rebel troops led by Moroccan commander, Mohammed el Mizzian, attacked the heights of the Sierra de Cavalls. The well-armed infantry had the support of 100 aircraft, and it took them one day to take the heights, causing tremendous Republican casualties (1,000 prisoners and 500 dead).[7] On 2 November the Nationalists occupied the Sierra de Pandols and on the following day they reached the river Ebro. They took Mora la Nova on 7 November, and by 10 November occupied Mount Picossa. The last Republican troops recrossed the Ebro at Flix on 16 November and the battle came to a close.[8]

The battle of the Ebro had been the longest battle of the Spanish Civil War, lasting 115 days, and had resulted in tremendous loss of weaponry and men, leaving the Republic in an impossibly vulnerable position. It had failed to stem the advance of the Nationalist Army and now its troops were tired, hungry, and war weary. There was a shortage of resources of all kinds, including food and war material.[9] Lillian made desperate pleas to the people back home in Britain:

> I have been doing medical work in Spain for 19 months, usually in the front line or in field dressing stations. I have seen the wonderful way in which the people are carrying on, and I cannot but admire their spirit and moral, but I have also seen how desperately they are in need. This is the third winter of the war and the women and children are lacking even the bare necessities of life. Some of the most needed things are food, soap, shoes and clothing [...] the cause of these people who are suffering through no fault of their own is a special and urgent one and becomes more urgent every day.[10]

Throughout the war, George Jeger had encouraged the volunteers to write letters about the work they were doing for the SMAC Bulletins. These would also occasionally be published in the British press in order to raise public awareness about the situation in Spain and to prompt donations towards medical aid. Jeger remarked that Lillian's letters were 'quiet sounding and shy at first' but later showed an aggressive streak. While she makes no attempt to deny this, she adds that, above all, they were 'always full of praise for the Spaniards we were working with'. Lillian was among the SMAC personnel remaining in Catalonia in the final days of the conflict. She writes to the Committee:

> Isn't it splendid the manner in which our Spanish army is resisting? You people in London can have no idea just how proud we nurses are, to be able to help and work, side by side with these Spanish comrades. [...] Since returning to Spain, I see more signs than before of the great sacrifices which these people are making. But one never hears a word to indicate just how weary they must be of this prolonged struggle for freedom. I speak with our young wounded comrades. They almost all speak of the hardships, etc., they endured in the early days of the war, when they were fleeing from the Fascists. They don't dwell much on these things [...] When I tell the men that we have so many more *camions* or shiploads of food being sent to Spain, they speak so feelingly and gratefully of the workers of England.[11]

However, while being interviewed after the war, thinking back about the brave Spanish people among whom she worked also triggered an unhappy memory for Lillian. Again, we are left to read between the lines for details of the event, but Lillian's anguish is clear:

> I was always ashamed that I slapped the face of that Spaniard because he was in a state of stress. I could escape and hopefully walk out of Spain if I wanted, but he was stuck there. I didn't know anything about his family. But he had nearly sliced my finger off—I mean the tomato soup all over us, especially me, was proof of that and me, a quick-tempered girl, a young girl, I did the slap and regretted it ever after.[12]

Thankfully, the story had a happy outcome and Lillian and the man in question became bosom friends. 'We were in the retreats together', explains Lillian, 'and he would do anything for me'.

La Retirada

Just over a month after the battle of the Ebro, on 23 December, Franco began the offensive on Catalonia and the *Sanidad Militar* ordered every available surgical équipe to the fronts. At that point, Lillian Urmston was with the XV Sanidad Army Corps near Valls.[13] Initially, there was hope that the front lines would be able to resist the Fascist attack, but it was soon evident that the enormous amount of war material at the disposal of the Fascists would make this impossible. For a disorganised army and a demoralised population, it proved too much. By 9 January, the rebels held a third of Catalan territory, taking 23,000 prisoners and killing 5,000 Republican soldiers.[14]

The *Sanidad* began the evacuation of the hospitals in Reus, Valls, Tarragona and Sabinosa to Vilafranca and Vilanova. This went on steadily for three weeks. Then, on Sunday 22 January came the order for the evacuation of the hospitals in Barcelona and the general evacuation of medical matériel and personnel to Gerona. The evacuation of hospitals, which had hitherto been carried out in quite an orderly fashion, now became chaotic. Large numbers of ambulances and trucks had been wrecked by bombings and shellings and although all reserves of vehicles were called upon for the evacuation of Barcelona, the number was insufficient. This meant that some hospitals were unable to be evacuated. Rosita Davson left the SMAC office in Barcelona with the Blood Transfusion Service. The office material was loaded onto trucks, but they would not be able to get out of Barcelona as an order was issued preventing any further vehicles from leaving the city.

The Nationalist aviation bombed Barcelona every day (40 times between 21 and 25 January). Realising that the end of the Republic was inevitable, many thousands of people fled north to France in what would become known as *la Retirada*. Together with Republican soldiers there were pitiful throngs of women and children, elderly and infirm, 'driven by physical or psychological fear of the last moments of a lost war.'[15] It is impossible to calculate the number of refugees that crossed the border into France. The most reliable (though conservative) estimate is probably that found in a report by the Préfet of the Eastern Pyrenees, which puts the number at about 480,000.[16] They were accompanied by members of the various humanitarian aid agencies that had been working in Barcelona—most notably, the Quakers. There were also SMAC volunteers, including Lillian Urmston.[17] All focused their efforts on helping refugees on their way into exile, providing hot food and medical care in improvised facilities along the roadside.[18] Lillian recalls:

> After the Ebro we were walking most of the time and setting up hospitals and the ambulances were delivering patients to the base hospitals as fast as we could [...] We would take over a house or we'd put up a tent by the roadside and you'd just got everything out and boiled and [were] feeling so proud that within two hours you were ready to operate and you'd just got your first casualties on the table and others were waiting and you had to pack up. But we did it quickly.

With the desperate shortage of ambulances, Lillian and her team once resorted to stealing a car from a commissar, and she made no secret of the offence. She deviates from her account of the *Retirada* to give details of the event (and to further explain her obvious dislike of commissars!)

> You probably gathered that quite a number of commissars I had no respect for. The only respect for commissars I had was when they downed their books and pamphlets and picked up rifles and bayonets and fought and they went up in my estimation [...] the British and American commissars were fighters like Bill Alexander you couldn't beat Bill for sheer guts and the Americans Oliver Law and

people like that [...] but others used to wander around and they had packets of cigars and cigarettes, and they would patronisingly say to a wounded man, 'Ho, you'll be alright in three days to take up a bayonet. You'll be alright.' And then they'd swagger out to their chauffeur-driven cars and I noticed they always had a comfortable mattress in the back of their cars and plenty of grub. I thought they should never have been commissars. In fact, I still felt that we didn't need commissars to boost up people's morale. I think that each individual had his own reserve of morale that could be called upon. The greater the crisis and the more severe the fighting the more tough everyone became. It was just automatic.[19]

The Nationalists finally occupied Barcelona on 26 January whereupon five days of looting and extrajudicial killings took place.[20] For some of the wounded, the old and infirm, there was no escape. 'Even though we knew the Nationalists were taking over,' lamented Lillian, 'we couldn't take them all into France, the French wouldn't receive them.' She describes the last, desperate journey she made into French territory:

we did finally do that last retreat on a truck, and we were going into France, we were laden with casualties, when you think of head wounds sitting up and amputations leaning on people, and we just crowded everyone into every *camion* and every ambulance we could.[21]

In the great confusion, some medical personnel lost all contact with their *équipes*, and *matériel* and ambulances were confiscated by the French authorities immediately the vehicles passed the frontier. The SMAC volunteers were advised to save as much material as possible, especially the autochirs, and send them to Valencia as soon as they were no longer needed in Perpignan. All further aid should be sent to

Valencia and consigned to the *Inspección General de Sanidad*, Refugee Camps.[22]

French concentration camps

When the French authorities, totally unprepared for such a human deluge, closed their border posts, thousands of people were left out in the open for several weeks, often in torrential rain and freezing temperatures. Quaker, Edith Pye writes from Perpignan:

> It is a really terrible tragedy here—till today the Pass leading to Spain has been one solid block of refugees, of all ages, wounded soldiers, etc., and I understand they spent the night standing, as one stands in the Tube in rush hours. They were prevented from coming into France by Senegalese soldiers. (They said, 'Moors behind us and now Moors in front!' and the crowd simply got wedged tighter and tighter.) Some of our people set up a canteen on the French side, giving a piece of bread and a drink of hot milk to all the women and children and old people [...] These poor people have absolutely no shelter—it poured in buckets all last night and thou can imagine what it was like.[23]

The French border was opened to women, children, and the elderly on 28 January 1939. The flood of refugees was now thirty miles long, stretching from La Junquera on the Spanish side to La Boulou and Argelès on the French side. The *Daily Telegraph* reports: 'There are at least 15,000 refugees waiting near Bourg-Madame and another 15,000 are in the vicinity of Le Perthus'.[24] By 2 February, more than 100,000 had entered the country. The border was finally opened to soldiers of the defeated republican army on 5 February, and more than 250,000 of them crossed into France before it was closed once again, on 15 February 1939, with the arrival of Franco's troops.

Although *la Retirada* came as no surprise to the French government, it had not foreseen the huge numbers of refugees involved. Provisions had been made for approximately 15,000 men (fleeing soldiers), and there were none at all for women, children, or the elderly. The men were herded into internment camps which were nothing more than vast open spaces along the sea shore, surrounded by barbed wire. There, on the windswept beaches, they were left to fend for themselves, as aid agencies were initially denied entry. About 170,000 women and children were distributed to hundreds of different locations around the country. The kind of welcome they received varied greatly, depending on the hospitality of the neighbours, the existing resources, and, above all, on the ideological affinity of the authorities.

More permanent camps were established at Argelès-sur-Mer, St Cyprien and Barcarès but the facilities were little better. Fierce winds and extreme temperatures further exacerbated the primitive conditions. After the scorching heat of the day, the night temperature dropped dramatically as strong winds from the sea whipped up the sand. Some men were able to build rudimentary shelters using driftwood and the bodywork of abandoned vehicles that were found in the vicinity of the camp, but very few had the luxury of a shelter and some of the weakest men froze to death overnight. Another serious problem was the lack of latrines, which meant that the men were forced to use the beach for all their bodily needs, thus adding unbearable filth to the cold, hunger, and thirst they had to endure. The water was not fit for consumption, and those who drank it fell prey to diarrhea and dysentery. There was such a lack of medical provision that dressings for wounds had to be repeatedly reused. Epidemics of scabies, whooping cough, measles, pneumonia, influenza, and typhoid fever were rampant. In the first six months, 14,672 refugees died from malnutrition or dysentery.[25] Lillian reported to the SMAC:

After 21 months' front-line nursing in Spain, one gets accustomed to all kinds of horrible sights, but the things seen during the last days of our retreat from Spain, and the experience undergone in the camp of St Cyprien near Perpignan, I shall never forget [...] Operating work was done, and efficiently, just inside houses which stood by the roadside. Many wounded, particularly refugees wounded in the many bombardments, were treated as they lay in the ditches, by the roadside. In innumerable instances we came upon families of refugees—parents and children, wounded whilst fleeing to safety. We cared for them and kept them with us if they were seriously wounded [...] Wounded men were without treatment for about six days. We were not allowed to tend our sick comrades. No hygienic arrangements had been made. One small spring supplied water for about 15,000-20,000 people.[26]

Initially, Lillian did not see the *Retirada* as the end for the Republic. 'Although sad at leaving our Spain,' she explained, 'we all realised that this had to be and looked forward to a rapid reorganisation in France which would result in our going back to another sector of Spain to carry on the struggle against Fascist aggression.'[27] However, after being held for several days in the St Cyprien camp she soon realized that her hopes for the future were not to be. Refugees were told: 'You have allowed yourselves to be expelled from your own homeland. Do not forget that this is France, and that here you have no right to anything.'[28] Strict (if not brutal) military discipline was imposed, and the internees viewed the camps not as a refuge but as a prison. If anyone attempted to breach the perimeter fence to go and seek food, they could expect violent reprisals. Typically, Lillian was determined to stand her ground:

I'd been treated as Russian because I wouldn't hand over my passport to the French and they kept telling me I was Russian, Rusky, and I belted a Frenchman for telling me that [...] I used to get money and go out for food because at a pinch I would have my passport.[29]

The attitude of the French authorities did little to allay the fears of the internees.[30] Albert Sarraut, the French Minister of the Interior, underlined the need to balance the humanitarian duty towards exiles with the maintenance of public order and the protection of French citizens. He declared that asylum seekers would be offered free passage back to Spain, where, if they were not criminals, they need have nothing to fear.[31] In some cases, forced repatriations would take place.[32]

The relief organisations provided help in the form of food, clothing, and medicines. Furthermore, they liaised with French officials to overcome their initial reaction of fear and revulsion in the face of the invading wave of displaced people. Many of the aid workers denounced the deplorable conditions. Dr Audrey Russell wrote: 'I wanted to cover my eyes, it was a sight that offended human dignity [...] men penned into cages like wild animals, or like cattle in the marketplace.'[33] British aristocrat, writer and social activist Nancy Cunard described her visit to the St Cyprien camp where Lillian Urmston was being kept:

> The scene there is more or less the same as in Argelès. One walks into a jumble of broken down cars and trucks. There are office files, tools, aircraft parts, machinery and the like everywhere [...] [T]here are dead donkeys everywhere; tonight the luckiest will eat them in the field. I saw how a stew was being made.[34]

However, not everyone was critical of the French authorities. British volunteer, Francesca Wilson, explains the dimensions and consequences of the refugee flood in the following terms:

> It was easy for the world, who were not faced by the same problem, to criticise the way in which the French dealt

with it. [...] The French Government was saddled with a burden which was an enormous strain on its housing capacity as well as its budget. The half a million refugees cost them at least £40,000 a day, but they would not accept money from our government (except through the Red Cross for clothing) because they did not want interference. Their intention was to send the Spaniards back as fast as possible; but many refused to go.[35]

This was what the internees feared, above all—being sent back to Spain, especially after hearing stories of repression and persecution from friends and relatives who had remained there. They begged the humanitarian agencies to help them avoid repatriation. Nevertheless, the policy of repatriation did lead to a considerable reduction in the number of internees in concentration camps from about 275,000 interned in February 1939, to 30,000 in April 1940.[36] The Spanish who were allowed asylum had to contribute to the national defence effort during the coming war. Some 40,000 Spaniards were employed in industry and agriculture, while about 55,000 joined the Foreign Workers Companies as labourers in public works, for example, in the maintenance of roads and railways and the construction of fortifications and trenches, etc. Some 6,000 enlisted in the Foreign Volunteer Marching Regiments (RMVE), military units made up of foreigners and affiliated with the Foreign Legion, and up to 1,000 in the latter. An additional factor in lowering the number of internees in the French camps was the emigration of almost 18,000 Spaniards to Latin American and European countries.[37]

Lillian spoke very highly of the work that the Quakers were doing in the camps. They provided invaluable material support in the form of milk for babies and children, food, clothing, medicines and financial aid. They also afforded crucial moral support to the internees and worked tirelessly to get as many people as they could out of the camps—be this into local employment or into the safety of another country.

None of this was easy—not least because of the enormous amount of bureaucracy it entailed, especially for those without papers. Lillian pleaded for the Quakers' help in homing two of the Spanish *chicas*, which they did, indeed, manage to do.

> to get those two girls back to England, I don't know whether they had to use bribery, which I fully anticipate [...] someone had to pay for papers, they had no papers [...] we had to vouch for the documentations, get them temporary passes as stateless people I suppose the Summerville family must have sent out for a start over a hundred pounds which in those days was a terrific amount of money.[38]

Lillian was reported missing, and a search was launched by the SMAC, with the help of the British Embassy. Rosita Davson heard that members of the XV Sanidad Army Corps had arrived in the French camps. 'I combed the camp for Lilian [sic] and found her,' she declares.[39] Lillian's reaction at being rescued was not what one might expect:

> And then Rosita came with this official and got me out. I had no choice in the matter but that was my second worst experience in my life leaving that camp with a group of people I'd gone through hell with, and they had to stay behind. I gave them everything I had except the rags I wore. They even had my watch—every little thing that was useful and I asked Rosita for cigarettes, she was a heavy smoker, I asked her for cigarettes to give them I asked the Consulate official and they just looked at me as if I was something out of a pig stye, which I probably was by that time and they wouldn't give a single cigarette and I was given a rousing farewell and that's when [...] it was when I got out of the cab that I just broke down and I just held up my eyes [...] it wasn't relief at being free it was sheer damn shame at leaving the people behind.[40]

Upon her arrival in England, Lillian was lodged in a flat near the Spanish Medical Aid Office where volunteers were still sorting out donated items to send on to the French concentration camps. She met up with some of the other nurses who had returned from Spain. However, with the exception of Nan Green, who had always shown her great kindness, Lillian declares: 'they weren't terribly friendly to me.' She was told by volunteer nurse, Mary Slater, that this was because people suspected she was a spy, as she was a member of the Territorial Army. As usual, Lillian formed her own opinion:

> I always felt that because I was not a member of the Communist Party I was slightly outside the magic circle, put it like that [...] I always thought that a lot of people wanted to join the Communist Party to get on the bandwagon.[41]

Chapter Ten:
Preparations in Britain for World War II

The coming war meant that Lillian's experience in Spain was of great value, and she was sought after to lecture on her wartime medical work.[1] Conscious of the need to secure paid employment, she took advantage of this opportunity which she also combined with continued fundraising on behalf of those Spanish refugees now interned in the French camps. One news report reads:

> A large audience gathered at Stanley Hall on Tuesday evening at a meeting arranged by the South Norwood and District Spanish Relief Committee. The speakers included Mr John Wilton (secretary, London Foodship Committee) Dr D E Barton MB, BS, Nurse Urmston (recently returned from Spain), Rev W R Devenish and others [...] Nurse Urmston gave a graphic account of the difficulties under which front line dressing stations and hospitals had to work and said that operations had to be performed with only the aid of local anaesthetics as no supplies were available, and the audience were made to feel the horror of the war, and the sufferings of the Spanish people, particularly the women and children, and a very generous response was made to an appeal for funds.[2]

Shortly afterwards, the *Bromley & West Kent Mercury* announced a meeting held by Petts Wood Committee for Spanish Relief at which Lillian was a speaker. It was declared that the Committee received support from people of 'all political creeds' in helping the Spanish people unite the forces of democracy against Fascism.

> Nurse Urmston said that though Franco was capturing Government territory it did not mean that he would ever

conquer the Spanish people [...] After describing the advance of Franco in Catalonia, she spoke of the five days she spent in a concentration camp. For the first four days, there were no rations. It was the duty of English people to see that supplies of food, clothing and medicine were sent to the people in Spain and in the concentration camps.[3]

The same newspaper later reported that Nurse Urmston had given a lecture to Bromley ARP Wardens at the Bromley County School for Boys. Her talk included special reference to air-raid precautions and the need for deep ARP shelters. 'The only real shelter is a deep one, 40ft below the surface of the ground. I am sorry we have not got them here, and I wish the Government would provide them,' declared Lillian. In an air raid, she explained, one's initial feeling was fear, 'but it was part of one's job to pretend not to be frightened'. She stressed that many lives were saved in Spain because people followed the wardens' instructions to enter the air raid shelters. She also warned those present that the bomb-droppers were 'jolly accurate,' thanks to the telescopic sights on the modern bomber plane. She told the reporter of the occasion when she was up at the front line during a bombardment and was thrown into a trench and buried by debris. Thankfully, she suffered only minor abrasions and when she was dug out, she was able to carry on with her work. The newspaper article concludes:

> With so many men away a great deal of ambulance work was done by boys and girls of 15, 16, and 17 years of age. With little training they went and put together broken humanity. By comparison she [nurse Urmston] felt disgusted at the attitude of many young people in England to National Defence. It was vitally necessary that everyone should train so that if war came to England everyone would be ready to step into a given post.[4]

During the following months, the press continued to report various such lectures on aspects of frontline medical care in Spain.[5] Lillian was also guest of honour at several public events including the 'spectacular Armistice Night Concert' staged by the ARP at Bolingbroke, Lincolnshire, to commemorate the opening of their enormous new air-raid shelter.[6]

Lillian was offered an advisory position with Battersea Council. Working alongside fellow SMAC volunteer, Dr Gerald Shirlaw, she trained council workers in first aid and wartime safety precautions and helped put in place measures for dealing with potential civilian casualties. At one point, she had what she called a 'dust up' with the Tory-controlled Town Hall when they declared that they would put a council member in charge of each first aid post. She voiced her absolute opposition to this, insisting that only medically qualified individuals should be considered for such a position, and received the full backing of Dr Shirlaw and of Dr MacDonald, the local Medical Officer of Health. 'I was adamant that not a single councillor would run a station as far as I was concerned,' declared Lillian, adding, after a moment's thought, 'there again, that might have been a throwback to political commissars because that was deeply embedded in me.'[7]

Once again, Gerald Shirlaw wrote a glowing report on the valuable work carried out by Lillian during the seven months period in which she was engaged in ARP work. Under Shirlaw's direction, she was responsible for much of the organisation, training, equipment, etc, of First Aid Posts and Stretcher Party Depots as well as for the training of those who offered their services prior to and during the early stages of the Second World War. 'She threw herself into this work with enthusiasm and zest,' adds Shirlaw. 'Nurse Urmston is one of the few nurses in England who has had a great deal of experience in modern casualty war service.'[8]

Lillian was then posted to northern France with the British Expeditionary Force (BEF), where her experience in Spain came in extremely useful. She advised nurses that as soon as air-raid warnings were sounded they should cover the heads of their patients with enamel bowls. This helped prevent splinters from causing head injuries. 'The patients' ears should be stopped with cotton wool,' she added, 'and they should each be given a piece of wood to bite on. A patient who is frightened naturally clenches his teeth. If he bites on the wood, it helps to prevent the ear drums from being shattered by the noise.'[9]

As the Germans swept across Belgium and France, in May and early June 1940, thousands of British Army personnel, including Lillian, were evacuated home to safety from Dunkirk and Boulogne. Many British Army nurses were eager to return to France, but were told to expect appointments, instead, to civilian hospitals in England. They protested at the British reluctance to allow women to go into the firing line. Unsurprisingly, Lillian's was one of the dissenting voices. The local newspaper reported an interview with her:

> 'Florence Nightingale and Edith Cavell faced danger at the front,' said a 26-year-old nurse from a hospital near Boulogne, 'and we modern young nurses are not afraid, either. I feel that our boys in France would like to be looked after by British nurses. I have appealed against the decision to send me to a civilian hospital. I want to be in the thick of things over there. I served in the Spanish War as a nurse with the Republican Army [...] After 22 months in Spain, dodging bombs and shell-fire all the time, my nerves are as tough as any man's. Many other nurses feel as I do—that the time has come to drop the old tradition that women should not be sent into the firing line.[10]

Lillian went on to serve as a nurse in Egypt, Syria, Sicily, and Anzio, Italy where she was badly injured by shell fire, suffering spinal injuries from which she never fully recovered. She met her future husband, John Buckoke, in the hospital where she was being treated. They married in in June 1945, in Cairo Cathedral.

Lillian never became involved in politics, though she was

made an honorary member of the Labour Party. Her allegiance was simply to the most vulnerable in society, the exploited and the oppressed. 'All through the war years, then when I went overseas where there was a so-called emergency—everywhere I worked I worked for the underdog,' she explains. She and her husband travelled to Kuala Lumpur where they helped the Chinese Indian survivors from the Death Railway.[11] Following that, Lillian helped prostitutes in Singapore to form a union. In later life she worked as a journalist for newspapers in Malaysia and wrote freelance for the *Daily Express* and *Daily Mail*. Lillian returned to Spain several times to visit the 'wonderful people' among whom she had lived and worked:

> The thing that impressed me most always was the sheer guts and courage of those Spaniards. Going through the second war afterwards and looking back I realize that even though I always admired the Spanish people tremendously, the courage they showed was something that I've never seen repeated in groups of people, however much they were shattered temporarily by bombings and losing their closest and not knowing where their husbands were, you could always rally them round and they made a supreme effort to help us with our wounded and everything and if anyone could ever wash clothes for us or cook something or do anything for us, regardless of nationalities, they would do it.[12]

While she went on to lead a full and adventurous life at home and abroad, after the Spanish Civil War, Lillian's most vivid and inspiring memories were clearly those of Spain. This had much to do with the Spanish people for whom she had a lasting admiration—and maybe just a little to do with the fact that in Spain she got to be something of a gypsy and a rebel.

Lillian passed away on 17 October 1990, aged 76, and was given a military funeral at St Margaret's Church, West Hoathly. Max Collin, volunteer ambulance driver in Spain, and colleague of Lillian in the British Medical Unit, learned of Lillian's passing in the press. He wrote:

> it is a measure of Lillian's modesty that I never knew of
> those perilous incidents in her life as mentioned in the
> paper [...] her courage was coupled with a humanity which
> manifested itself in the loving attention she gave to those
> she served.[13]

A blue plaque celebrating Lillian's life and achievements was
unveiled in Tameside on 6 March 2008. The plaque adorns
the façade of St Paul's Primary School, Huddersfield Road,
Stalybridge, where Lillian was a pupil.

Appendix

Ministry of Defence, 24 October 1985

Sister Lilian [sic] Buckoke (P215631) Territorial Army Nursing Services

The military services of the above-named officer is as follows:

Enrolled into Territorial Army Nursing Services   5. 8. 36

Joined 18th Hospital for duty   30. 1. 40

Granted Emergency Commission   30. 5. 41

Relegated to unemployed list   17. 9. 46

She relinquished her commission on 1. 3. 51 and was granted the honorary rank of Sister.

Served overseas:

    BEF France   27. 4. 40-21. 5. 40

    Middle East Command   22. 4. 41-25. 10. 45

Yours sincerely,

J. E. Treble[1]

ENGLISH NURSE IN SPAIN

IV.—On the Teruel Front

LILLIAN URMSTON, S.R.N., T.A.N.S., an English nurse who spent 22 months nursing in the front line in Spain, describes her adventures in a series of articles specially written for the NURSING MIRROR. This week she tells of shrapnel casualties, frost-bite wounds, and how she had to be cook as well as nurse

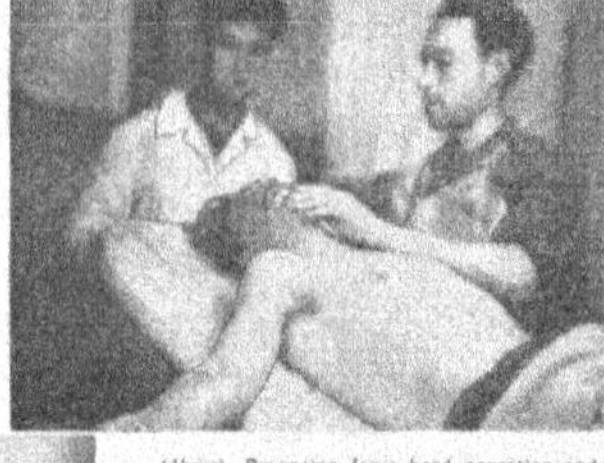

(Above) Preparing for a head operation and (left) Miss Urmston assisting Dr. Broggi in the operating room.

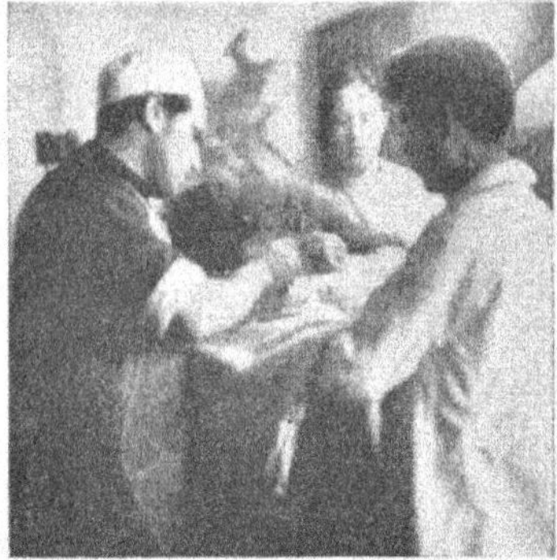

THE cases we received on the Spanish front had chiefly shrapnel and bullet wounds. In the rearguard, the majority of casualties were from shrapnel. In the small towns and villages, between the front line and the rearguard, we frequently had civilians, besides soldiers, who had, for the most part, shrapnel wounds. Sometimes, especially in the cases of families of refugees, who were fleeing along the roads, enemy planes would swoop down and "strafe" with a machine-gun the helpless people. I did not often come across cases of burns from incendiary bombs. In Spain, these caused comparatively little damage, both to the population and to the buildings.

Once I looked after a wounded aviator. His plane had been brought down, and the tank had exploded. He had fairly deep and extensive wounds of head, chest and abdomen, besides multiple fractures. Despite the prompt shock treatment that was administered, he died within two hours.

Another case I well remember was in September, 1937. A chauffeur was brought in. His vehicle had, I think, collided with another, again the petrol tank had exploded and fired, and he was admitted into hospital suffering from a fractured femur and burns on the hands, lower abdomen and upper part of the leg. Luckily, we had a radiant heat apparatus, and so used that immediately. He was given an injection of camphor and caffeine, followed a little later by a 300 c.c. intravenous injection of glucosade. He also had an injection of morphia. As he responded very well to this treatment, the surgeon was able, quite soon, to put up his leg, using a Böhler splint. As we did not have a gas and oxygen apparatus, we had to use ether for the anæsthetic.

I thoroughly cleaned the wound with a solution of soap and water, then mopped over the burned area with a swab dipped in methylated spirits, and then with ether. We had no tannic acid in any form, so reverted to picric acid ($\frac{1}{2}$% solution). We soaked strips of gauze in this and laid them lightly over the area. This was bandaged lightly but firmly, using triangular bandage. I cannot say the wounds received the correct routine treatment. Sometimes the dressings were renewed every three hours; other times, owing to the extreme pressure of work, five hours would elapse before the dressings were renewed. After just more than three weeks, the burns were almost healed. We then applied, *twice* each day, a dressing which was frequently used in Spain; a special gauze which

11. One of a series of articles on medical work in Spain that Lillian wrote for the *Nursing Mirror* (1939). (Wellcome Collection, London.)

12. With the ARP in Battersea,
London, January 1940 (1).

13. With the ARP,
Battersea (2).

14. With the ARP in Battersea, London, January 1940 (3).
Lillian on far right with child.

15. Lillian marries John Buckoke in Cairo Cathedral, 23 June 1945.

List of Illustrations and Sources

Unless otherwise stated, the photographs listed are from the papers of Lillian Urmston, courtesy of the Museum of Military Medicine, Aldershot, UK.

Page 6:

1. Lillian in nurse's uniform (unknown location) c.1937.

Pages 63-64:

2. Lillian with Dorothy Low and Spanish driver, Enrique. Lérida, August 1937.
3. From right to left, Lillian, Irene Goldin and Dorothy Rutter, Quinto, October 1937.
4. From right to left, Lillian, Keith (Andy) Andrews, Dorothy Rutter and Leah Manning with British, American and Spanish orderlies, Cedrillas (Teruel).
5. Lillian and driver with ambulance at Cedrillas (Teruel).
6. With American Brigader Norman Dorland, at Alcorisa. Dorland was wounded at the battle of Brunete at the end of July 1937, while serving with the XV Brigade.

Pages 115-116:

7. The British press report on Lillian's medical work in Spain.
8. Lilian entering the Santa Lucía cave hospital on the Ebro front, July 1938.
9. Lillian with the Dutch commissar in the cave hospital. [Courtesy of the Noel Butlin Archives Centre, Australian

National University: Phil Thorne Collection, P15-31-21, Photograph of Ebro offensive – Nurse Lilian Urmston speaks with a wounded soldier, July 1938.]
10. The Dutch commissar enjoys a cigarette.

Pages 141-142:

11. One of a series of articles on medical work in Spain that Lillian wrote for the *Nursing Mirror* (1939). [Courtesy of the Wellcome Collection, London.]
12. With the ARP in Battersea, London, January 1940 (1).
13. With the ARP, Battersea (2).
14. With the ARP in Battersea, London, January 1940 (3). Lillian on far right with child.
15. Lillian marries John Buckoke in Cairo Cathedral, 23 June 1945.

References

Alexander, Bill, *British Volunteers for Liberty: Spain 1936-1939,* (London: Lawrence & Wishart Ltd, 1982).

Alted Vigil, Alicia, 'Humanitarian aid: From the Spanish Civil War to the early days of post-war Europe'. *Culture & History Digital Journal*, 2019; 8 (2).

Alted, Alicia. *La voz de los vencidos. El exilio republicano de 1939.* Madrid: Aguilar, 2005.

Bastos Ansart, Manuel, *Las heridas por arma de fuego* (Barcelona: Editorial Labor S.A., 1936).

Antony Beevor, *The Battle for Spain. The Spanish Civil War, 1936–1939,* (London: Penguin Books, 2006).

Blanc Fortacín, J., and M. Martínez Piñeiro, 'Curso de transfusión de sangre', *El Siglo Médico* 1927; 79: 171-2; 207-10; 240-4; 270-2; 302-8; 329-32; 355-8; 383-5.

Broggi, Moisès, *Memorias de un cirujano (1908–1945),* (Barcelona: Ediciones Península, 2001).

Baxell, Richard, *Unlikely Warriors. The British in the Spanish Civil War and the struggle against fascism,* (London: Aurum Press Ltd., 2012).

_________, *British Volunteers in the Spanish Civil War,* (Pontypool: Warren and Pell, 2007).

Buchanan, Tom, *Britain and the Spanish Civil War* (Cambridge, 1997).

__________, *The Impact of the Spanish Civil War on Britain: War, Loss and Memory* (Eastbourne, 2017).

Casañ, Guillermo, 'El hospital de Benicàssim en el contexto del Servicio sanitario de las brigadas internacionales (Guerra Civil, 1936–1939)' in Manuel Requena Gallego y Rosa María Sepúlveda Losa (coord.), *La sanidad en las Brigadas Internacionales* (Cuenca: Ediciones de la Universidad de Castilla–La Mancha, 2006).

Coni, Nicolas, *Medicine and Warfare: Spain, 1936-1939*, (Routledge/Canada Blanch Studies on Contemporary Spain, 2008).

Corkill, David and Stuart J. Rawnsley, *The road to Spain: anti-fascists at war, 1936-1939*, (Dunfermline: Borderline, 1981).

d'Harcourt Got, Jouaquín, in *Revista de Sanidad de Guerra*, Nº 8, a monograph dedicated to the Blood Transfusion Service of the Republic, (Barcelona, Jefatura de Sanidad del Ejército, December 1937).

Duran Jordà, Federico, 'El Servicio de Transfusión de Sangre de Barcelona: Técnicas y utillaje', *Revista Sanidad de Guerra*, Año 1, Nº 8, December 1937.

Fillol, Vicente, *Los Perdedores: Memorias de un exiliado español*, (Madrid: Ediciones 'Gaceta Ilustrada', 1973).

Franco Grande, Avelino, Julián Álvarez Escudero and Joaquín Cortés Laíño, *Historia de la Anestesia en España 1847-1940*, (Madrid: Arán Ediciones S.L., 2005).

Fyrth, Jim, *The Signal was Spain: The Aid Spain Movement in Britain, 1936–39,* (London: Lawrence and Wishart, 1986).

Fyvel, Penelope, *English Penny*, (Ilfracombe, Devon: Arthur H. Stockwell, 1992).

Fyrth, Jim, and Sally Alexander, *Women's Voices from the Spanish Civil War*, (London: Lawrence and Wishart, 1991).

Green, Nan, *A Chronicle of Small Beer: The Memoirs of Nan Green*, (Nottingham: Trent Editions, 2004).

Handley, Sasha, Rohan McWilliam and Lucy Noakes (eds.), *New Directions in Social and Cultural History*, (London: Bloomsbury Academic, 2018).

Hervás Puyal, Carles, 'The organisation of combat casualty care in the Republican Army', in Josep Sánchez Cervelló and Pere Clua Micola (eds), *The battle of the Ebro: A river of blood*. (Special 80th Anniversary Edition, Consorsi Memorial dels Espais de la Batalla de l'Ebre (COMEBE), 2018).

Hoffer, Eric, *The True Believer*. (Harper Perennial Modern Classics, 2010), p. 302.

Iordache Cârstea, Luiza, 'Españoles tras las alambradas. Republicanos en los campos franceses, nazis y soviéticos (1939-1956)'. *Hispania Nova*, 1, 2019, pp. 27-28.

Jackson, Angela, *British Women and the Spanish Civil War*, (London: Routledge, 2002).

Jolly, Douglas, *Field Surgery in Total War*, (London: Hamish Hamilton, 1941).

Larraz, P., and C. Ibarrola, 'Los pies de Teruel: Asistencia y tratamiento de las heridas por congelación en los hospitales navarros durante la guerra civil'. Extract published on the Internet; date unknown:

http://www.requetes.com/sanidad.html.

Manning, Leah, *A Life for Education. An Autobiography*, (Gollancz: London, 1970).

Martín-Moruno, Dolores, 'Tejiendo redes de cuidado. La compasión como conocimiento de las mujeres humanitarias en la guerra (1853–1945).' In A. Zarzoso and J. Arrizabalaga (eds.), *Al servicio de la salud humana. La historia de la medicina ante los retos del siglo XXI*. Ciudad Real: QL Printers, 2017, pp. 21-26.

__________, 'Las enfermeras suizas de los trenes de prisioneros durante la Gran Guerra.' In A. Zarzoso and J. Arrizabalaga(eds.), *Al servicio de la salud humana. La historia de la medicina ante los retos del siglo XXI*, 21–26. Ciudad Real: QL Printers, 2017, pp. 177–182.

Mason, Emily, *Democracy, Deeds and Dilemmas: Support for the Spanish Republic Within British Civil Society, 1936–1939*, (Brighton: Sussex Academic Press, 2018).

Mates, Lewis H., *The Spanish Civil War and the British Left: Political Activism and the Popular Front*, (Tauris Academic Studies, 2008).

Molinero, Carme, Margarita Sala and Jaume Sobrequés, (eds.), *Una inmensa prisión. Los campos de concentración y las prisiones durante la guerra civil y el franquismo*, (Barcelona: Crítica, 2003).

Munté-Mateu, Josep, 'L'hospital del Mas de Santa Magdalena (Mora d'Ebre)'. *Miscellània del CERE* 31 (2021).

Navarro Carballo, José Ramón, *La Sanidad en las Brigadas Internacionales* (Madrid: Servicio de Publicaciones del

Estado Mayor del Ejército, 1989).

Palfreeman, Linda, *Salud! British Volunteers in the Republican Medical Service during the Spanish Civil War, 1936-1939*, (Cañada Blanch/Sussex Academic Studies on Contemporary Spain, 2012).

Preston, Paul, *A Concise History of the Spanish Civil War*, (Fontana Press, 1996); *The Spanish Civil War: Reaction, Revolution and Revenge*, (William Collins, 2016).

__________, *The Spanish Holocaust*, (London: HarperCollins Publishers Ltd, 2008).

__________, *The Coming of the Spanish Civil War: Reform, Reaction and Revolution in the Second Republic* (second edition, Routledge, London, 1994).

Rees, Richard, *A Theory of My Time. An Essay in Didactic Reminiscence.* (London: Secker & Warburg, 1963).

Requena Gallego, Manuel, and Rosa María Sepúlveda Losa (coord.), *La sanidad en las Brigadas Internacionales.* (Cuenca: Ediciones de la Universidad de Castilla–La Mancha, 2006).

Rubin, Hank, *Spain's Cause was Mine: A Memoir of an American Medic in the Spanish Civil War*, (Southern Illinois University Press, 1997).

Ruivenkamp, Evert, *Een Hollandse jongen aan de Ebro—Dagboek van een Spanjestrijder*, (Uitgeverij Jurgen Maas, 2022).

Sánchez Cervelló, Josep, and Pere Clua Micola (eds), *The battle of the Ebro: A river of blood.* (Special 80th Anniversary

Edition, Consorsi Memorial dels Espais de la Batalla de l'Ebre (COMEBE), 2018).

Shirlaw, G. B., *Casualty: Training, Organisation and Administration of Civil Defence Casualty Services*. (London: Secker and Warburg, 1940).

Shirlaw, G. B. and C. Troke, *Medicine versus invasion: the Home Guard Medical Service in Action*. (London: Secker and Warburg, 1941).

Sinclair-Loutit, Kenneth, *Very Little Luggage*: http://www.spartacus.schoolnet.co.uk/Loutit1.htm.

Skoutelsky, Rém,i *Novedad en el Frente. Las Brigadas Internacionales en la Guerra Civil,* (Madrid: Ediciones Temas de Hoy, S.A., 2006).

Summerfield, Penny, 'Subjectivity, the Self and Historical Practice.' In Sasha Handley, Rohan McWilliam and Lucy Noakes (eds.), *New Directions in Social and Cultural History*. (London: Bloomsbury Academic, 2018), pp. 21-44.

Thomas, Hugh, *The Spanish Civil War*, (Penguin; 4th edition, 2003).

Trueta, Josep, *Treatment of War Wounds and Fractures*. (London: Hamilton, 1939).

Tuban, Grégory, *Camps d'étrangers: le contrôle des réfugiés venus d'Espagne (1939-1944)*, (París: Nouveau Monde Éditions, 2018).

Valls, Roser, (coord.), *Infermeres catalanes a la Guerra Civil española*, (Barcelona: Publicacions i Edicions Universidad de Barcelona, 2008).

Vilanova i Vila-Abadal, Francesc, 'En el exilio: de los campos franceses al umbral de la deportación'. In Molinero, Carme, Sala, Margarita and Sobrequés, Jaume (eds.). *Una inmensa prisión. Los campos de concentración y las prisiones durante la guerra civil y el franquismo.* (Barcelona: Crítica, 2003), pp. 85-87.

Vogel, Sidney, 'Voices from the Past', *American Journal of Public Health*, December 2008, Vol. 98, No. 12, pp. 2148-2149.

Wilson, Francesca, *In the Margins of Chaos. Recollections of Relief Work in and between Three Wars,* (London: John Murray, 1944).

Zarzoso, Alfons, and Jon Arrizabalaga(eds.), *Al servicio de la salud humana. La historia de la medicina ante los retos del siglo XXI*, 21–26. Ciudad Real: QL Printers, 2017, pp. 177-182.

Notes

Notes to Preface

1 The 35th Medical Division was attached to the French Battalion the XIV International Brigade.

Notes to Introduction

1 For comprehensive accounts of the Spanish Civil War, see, for example, Hugh Thomas, *The Spanish Civil War*, (Penguin; 4th edition, 2003); or the books of Paul Preston: *A Concise History of the Spanish Civil War*, (Fontana Press, 1996); *The Spanish Civil War: Reaction, Revolution and Revenge*, (William Collins, 2016).

2 Richard Baxell, *Unlikely Warriors. The British in the Spanish Civil War and the struggle against fascism*, (London: Aurum Press Ltd., 2012).

3 Jim Fyrth, *The Signal was Spain: The Aid Spain Movement in Britain, 1936-39,* (London: Lawrence and Wishart, 1986) p. 21.

4 Tom Buchanan, *Britain and the Spanish Civil War* (Cambridge, 1997); and Tom Buchanan, *The Impact of the Spanish Civil War on Britain: War, Loss and Memory* (Eastbourne, 2017).

5 For a more nuanced analysis of local and regional responses to the conflict by the left in England, see Lewis H. Mates, *The Spanish Civil War and the British Left: Political Activism and the Popular Front*, (Tauris Academic Studies, 2008).

6 Emily Mason, *Democracy, Deeds and Dilemmas: Support for the Spanish Republic Within British Civil Society, 1936-1939,*

(Brighton: Sussex Academic Press, 2018).

7 Dolores Martín-Moruno, 'Tejiendo redes de cuidado. La compasión como conocimiento de las mujeres humanitarias en la guerra (1853-1945).' In A. Zarzoso and J. Arrizabalaga (eds.), *Al servicio de la salud humana. La historia de la medicina ante los retos del siglo XXI*. Ciudad Real: QL Printers, 2017, pp. 21-26. Dolores Martín-Moruno, 'Las enfermeras suizas de los trenes de prisioneros durante la Gran Guerra.' In A. Zarzoso and J. Arrizabalaga(eds.), *Al servicio de la salud humana. La historia de la medicina ante los retos del siglo XXI*, 21-26. Ciudad Real: QL Printers, 2017, pp. 177-182.

8 See, for example, works by the various male colleagues with whom Lillian worked in Spain, including: Douglas Jolly, Field Surgery in Total War. (London: Hamish Hamilton, 1941); Josep Trueta, *Treatment of War Wounds and Fractures*. (London: Hamilton, 1939); G. B. Shirlaw, *Casualty: Training, Organisation and Administration of Civil Defence Casualty Services*. (London: Secker and Warburg, 1940); Gerald B. Shirlaw and C. Troke, *Medicine versus invasion: the Home Guard Medical Service in Action*. (London: Secker and Warburg, 1941.)

9 Penny Summerfield, 'Subjectivity, the Self and Historical Practice.' In Sasha Handley, Rohan McWilliam and Lucy Noakes (eds.), *New Directions in Social and Cultural History*. (London: Bloomsbury Academic, 2018), pp. 21-44.

10 Held in the Museum of Military Medicine, Aldershot.

11 Held in the Wellcome Collection, London.

12 David Corkill and Stuart J. Rawnsley, *The road to Spain: anti-fascists at war, 1936-1939*. (Dunfermline: Borderline, 1981.)

13 The Tameside Local Studies Centre in Ashton-under-Lyne holds 114 tapes of interviews of International Brigaders and

volunteers in the aid-Spain movement.

14 See, for example, Linda Palfreeman, *Salud! British Volunteers in the Republican Medical Service during the Spanish Civil War, 1936-1939*, (Cañada Blanch/Sussex Academic Studies on Contemporary Spain, 2012); Nicolas Coni, *Medicine and Warfare: Spain, 1936-1939*, (Routledge/Canada Blanch Studies on Contemporary Spain, 2008).

Notes to Chapter One

1 Lillian Buckoke (née Urmston), the Manchester Studies interviews at Tameside Local Studies Centre. The interview forms the basis of this chapter, covering Lillian's early life, and is the source of all her quoted words. All references to the interview in subsequent chapters are given as 'Urmston, Tameside'.

2 Cade earned a reputation for defending the rights of the ordinary citizen and for fighting against corruption, maladministration, and abuse of power in both local and central governments.

3 Eric Hoffer, *The True Believer*. (Harper Perennial Modern Classics, 2010), p. 302.

4 Though Lillian did not, at that point, articulate it as such, this event would appear to indicate a growing awareness of the restraints of gender on admittance into the professional and public sphere—a legacy of the Victorian era from which she would do her best to shake free.

5 The young nurse in question suffered a breakdown after the death of her fiancé but eventually returned to duty. She was late in taking her exams, however, and she and Lillian parted ways.

Notes to Chapter Two

1 For a detailed explanation of events leading up to the military coup of 1936, see Paul Preston, *The Coming of the Spanish Civil War: Reform, Reaction and Revolution in the Second Republic* (second edition, Routledge, London, 1994).

2 See Richard Baxell, *British Volunteers in the Spanish Civil War*, (Pontypool: Warren and Pell, 2007).

3 For a comprehensive account of the British Aid to Spain movement and of the work of the Spanish Medical Aid Committee, see Jim Fyrth, *The Signal was Spain* (London: Lawrence and Wishart, 1986). See also Tom Buchanan, *Britain and the Spanish Civil War* (Cambridge University Press, 1997). Angela Jackson offers a brief summary of groups and associations formed to organise medical aid to Spain, in *British Women and the Spanish Civil War*, (London: Routledge, 2002), pp. 245-250.

4 Tom Buchanan, *Britain and the Spanish Civil War* (Cambridge University Press, 1997), p. 3.

5 Isabel Brown trained as a teacher. She joined the Labour Party and became an active member of the National Union of Teachers. She was later founder member of the Communist Party of Great Britain (CPGB). After studying at the Lenin School, she became leader of the British Committee for the Relief of Victims of Fascism.

6 The communist involvement in the SMAC is discussed by members of the medical unit in Spain. See, for example: Kenneth Sinclair-Loutit, *Very Little Luggage*. Published by David Loutit, 2021.

7 The TUC would eventually withdraw its financial support from the SMAC when it became clear that the Committee could not (or would not) remove its controlling Communist elements.

8 Lillian firmly believed that it was her lack of political affiliation (in particular, to the Communist Party) that prevented her from 'fitting in' entirely with her colleagues in the SMAC.

9 Leah Manning, *A Life for Education. An Autobiography*, (Gollancz: London, 1970), p. 75.

10 Nan Green, *A Chronicle of Small Beer: The Memoirs of Nan Green*, (Nottingham: Trent Editions), 2004, p. 73.

11 The resentment caused by the role of the Communist Party in the SMAC is also discussed in Tom Buchanan, *Britain and the Spanish Civil War* (Cambridge University Press, 1977), p. 102.

12 Urmston, Tameside.

13 Urmston, Tameside.

14 Linda Palfreeman, *Salud! British Volunteers in the Republican Medical Service during the Spanish Civil War, 1936–1939.* (The Cañada Blanch / Sussex Academic Studies on Contemporary Spain, 2012), p. 30.

15 See, for example, Rosita Davson (and signed by several members of the SMAC Unit in Grañén), 'Memorandum No.1', 30 November 1936. Archives of the Trades Union Congress, Warwick Digital Library (from hereon, WDL) 292/946/41/11(vii).

16 Buchanan 2017, p. 45.

17 Urmston, Tameside.

Notes to Chapter Three

1 Urmston, Tameside.

2 Davson was in charge of the SMAC flat in Barcelona. She acted

as interpreter and supply administrator. She was not very popular among the SMAC volunteers, some of whom thought she might be a spy.

3 The Thaelmann Battalion comprised mainly German Communists. During the early days of the conflict, a few British Brigaders (as the Tom Mann Centuria) were attached to it.

4 *Practicantes* were medical assistants. They could assist in surgical interventions and in childbirth, and also carry out minor surgery under the instruction of a doctor. They were experts in giving injection and in wound dressing.

5 Urmston, Tameside.

6 This did cause some friction between the majority of the group and some individuals who were against the Unit becoming subject to military rule.

7 Linda Palfreeman, *SALUD! British Volunteers in the Republican Medical Service during the Spanish Civil War, 1936-1939*, 2011, p. 4.

8 José Ramón Navarro Carballo, *La Sanidad en las Brigadas Internacionales* (Madrid: Servicio de Publicaciones del Estado Mayor del Ejército, 1989), pp. 233-238.

9 Rudolf Neumann, in Guillermo Casañ, 'El hospital de Benicàssim en el contexto del Servicio sanitario de las brigadas internacionales (Guerra Civil, 1936-1939)' in Manuel Requena Gallego y Rosa María Sepúlveda Losa (coord.), *La sanidad en las Brigadas Internacionales* (Cuenca: Ediciones de la Universidad de Castilla-La Mancha, 2006), pp. 161-197.

10 Navarro Carballo, 1989, p. 78

11 Douglas Jolly, Field Surgery in Total War (London: Hamish Hamilton, 1941), preface, xii.

12 Moisès Broggi, *Memorias de un cirujano (1908–1945)*, (Barcelona: Ediciones Península, 2001), p. 203.

13 Interview with Charlie Innocent, IWM Sound Archives, accession no. 13790.

14 Lillian Urmston, 'An English Nurse in Spain', *Nursing Mirror*, 27 May 1939, p. 293.

15 Manuel Bastos Ansart, *Las heridas por arma de fuego* (Barcelona: Editorial Labor S.A., 1936).

16 After the fall of Barcelona, Trueta crossed the Pyrenees into France on foot, later settling in England. He took up the post of Assistant Surgeon at the Wingfield-Morris Orthopaedic Hospital in Oxford and Head Surgeon of the Accident Service at the Radcliffe Infirmary. Most notably, Trueta published *Treatment of War Wounds and Fractures*, (London: Hamilton, 1939), which was later translated into various languages.

17 See Jolly 1941, pp. 227-226.

Notes to Chapter Four

1 Lillian Urmston, 'An English Nurse in Spain', *Nursing Mirror*, 13 May 1939 p. 231.

2 Douglas Jolly, *Field Surgery in Total War*, (London: Hamish Hamilton, 1941), p. 31.

3 Lillian Urmston, 'An English Nurse in Spain: Training nurses in the battle line', *Nursing Mirror*, 24 June 1939, p. 435.

4 Lillian Urmston, 'An English Nurse in Spain', *Nursing Mirror*, 13 May 1939 p. 231

5 *Ibid.*

6 *Ibid.*

7 Lillian Urmston, 'An English Nurse in Spain: Travelling in Convoy', *Nursing Mirror*, 27 May 1939, p. 293.

8 Lillian Urmston, 'An English Nurse in Spain: Training nurses in the battle line', *Nursing Mirror*, 24 June 1939, p 435.

9 Moisés Broggi, 2001, p. 203.

10 Lillian Urmston, 'An English Nurse in Spain: Training nurses in the battle line', *Nursing Mirror*, 24 June 1939, 17 June 1939, p. 403.

11 Lillian Urmston, 'An English Nurse in Spain: Travelling in convoy', *Nursing Mirror*, 27 May 1939, p. 293.

12 Lillian Urmston, 'An English Nurse in Spain: Travelling in convoy', *Nursing Mirror*, 27 May 1939, p. 293. Lillian could be referring to the small town of Gelsa, near Quinto.

13 There were important developments made in the field of nursing, in Spain, during the period of the Second Republic. Thanks to a grant from the Rockefeller Foundation, between 1931 and 1936, 14 Catalan nurses went to the USA to complete a course of postgraduate training in Public Healthcare, before taking up positions of responsibility in future centres for the training of nurses in Spain. One of the most ambitious projects of the Catalan government towards the professionalisation of nursing was the foundation of the third nursing school, l'Escola d'Infemeres de la Generalitat republicana. For further discussion, see Roser Valls (coord.), *Infermeres catalanes a la Guerra Civil española*, (Barcelona: Publicacions i Edicions Universidad de Barcelona, 2008).

14 The unqualified assistant was referred to as a *chica*—meaning 'girl' in Spanish.

15 Lillian Urmston, 'An English Nurse in Spain: Travelling in convoy', *Nursing Mirror*, 27 May 1939, p. 293.

16 It is unclear exactly when, or even if, Prime Minister Francisco Largo Caballero gave the order for the removal of women from the fighting militia. However, their withdrawal began as early as September 1936.

17 Urmston, Tameside.

18 Lillian Urmston, 'An English Nurse in Spain: Training nurses in the battle line', *Nursing Mirror*, 24 June, p. 436.

19 Lillian Urmston, 'An English Nurse in Spain: Training nurses in the battle line', *Nursing Mirror*, 24 June, p. 436.

20 Rule 25. Medical personnel exclusively assigned to medical duties must be respected and protected in all circumstances. They lose their protection if they commit, outside their humanitarian function, acts harmful to the enemy. This rule goes back to the 1864 Geneva Convention and was repeated in the subsequent Geneva Conventions of 1906 and 1929. International Humanitarian Law Databases: https://ihl-databases.icrc.org/en/customary-ihl/v1/rule25.

21 Kenneth Sinclair-Loutit, Very Little Luggage: http://www.spartacus.schoolnet.co.ukgrara/Loutit1.htm.

22 Urmston, Tameside.

23 Captain Strauss served with the XV Brigade. He was Battalion Doctor with the Washington Battalion and the Lincoln-Washington Battalion, later becoming Chief of XV Medical Services.

24 Urmston, Tameside.

25 Urmston, Tameside.

26 Sadly, like others, Broggi remembers the name of the 'very beautiful' Patience, who worked with Tudor Hart, but not that of Lillian, his own theatre nurse.

27 In Fyrth, *The Signal Was Spain: The Aid Spain Movement in Britain, 1936–39.* (London: Lawrence and Wishart, 1986), p. 98.

Notes to Chapter Five

1 Lillian Urmston, 'An English Nurse in Spain: Wounds and infections', *Nursing Mirror*, 20 May 1939, p. 273.

2 D.W. Jolly, *Field Surgery in Total War*, (London: Hamish Hamilton, 1940).

3 Penelope Fyvel, *English Penny*, (Ilfracombe, Devon: Arthur H. Stockwell, 1992), pp. 27-29.

4 Alexander Tudor Hart, Interview for IWM, accession number 13771.

5 Lillian Urmston, 'An English Nurse in Spain: Wounds and Infections', *Nursing Mirror*, 20 May 1939, p. 273.

6 Lillian Urmston, 'An English Nurse in Spain: Wounds and Infections', *Nursing Mirror*, 20 May 1939, p. 273.

7 *Ibid.*

8 *Ibid.*

9 *Ibid.*

10 Lillian Urmston, 'An English Nurse in Spain: Wounds', *Nursing Mirror*, 3 June 1939, pp. 335-336.

11 Dr Joaquín d'Harcourt Got, in the prologue to the research journal *Revista de Sanidad de Guerra*, Nº 8, a monograph

dedicated to the Blood Transfusion Service of the Republic, (Barcelona, Jefatura de Sanidad del Ejército), December 1937. The monograph comprises nine articles—four of them written by Duran and the rest by his collaborators.

12 Lillian Urmston, 'An English Nurse in Spain: Wounds and Infections', *Nursing Mirror*, 20 May 1939, p. 273.

13 Sidney Vogel, 'Voices from the Past', *American Journal of Public Health*, December 2008, Vol. 98, No. 12, pp. 2148-2149.

14 Lillian Urmston, 'An English Nurse in Spain: Haemorrhage and Shock', *Nursing Mirror*, 10 June 1939, p. 369.

15 *Ibid.*

16 *Ibid.*

17 *Ibid.*

18 The use of sodium citrate as an anticoagulant for blood was developed during 1914-1915, by various researchers working independently: Albert Hustin in Belgium, Luis Agote in Argentina, and Richard Lewisohn in New York.

19 The first course on blood transfusion was carried out at the Hospital de la Princesa in Madrid, by doctors José Blanc Fortacín and Martínez Piñeiro, in 1927. The course was subsequently published in *El Siglo Médico*: J. Blanc Fortacín and M. Martínez Piñeiro, 'Curso de transfusión de sangre', *El Siglo Médico* 1927; 79: 171-2; 207-10; 240-4; 270-2; 302-8; 329-32; 355-8; 383-5. In Avelino Franco Grande, Julian Álvarez Escudero and Joaquín Cortés Laíño, *Historia de la Anestesia en España 1847-1940*, (Madrid: Arán Ediciones S.L., 2005), Chapter 16, 'Historia de la transfusión sanguínea en España (1874-1940)', pp. 227-242.

20 The precedent for this kind of institution had been established on a much smaller scale by Percy Lane Oliver in Britain in 1921, in conjunction with the Red Cross.

21 Due to the lack of raw materials with which to carry out the specific test required, the donor was often simply asked to testify that they had never suffered from malaria.

22 El *Diari de Barcelona* 15 July 1937.

23 Dr Federico Duran i Jordà, 'El Servicio de Transfusión de Sangre de Barcelona: Técnicas y utillaje', *Revista Sanidad de Guerra*, Año 1, Nº 8, December 1937.

24 Spanish Medical Aid Committee Bulletin, 31 July 1938, Archives of the Trades Union Congress, (WDL 292/946/42/15(ii)).

25 Leah Manning, Spanish Medical Aid Committee, Report on International Conference for Medical Aid to Spain, 31 July 1938. WDL 292/946/42/15(ii).

26 These were supplied free of charge, along with other material, by the company Laboratori Químic Biològic Pelayo. The container held a capacity of 300 c.c. of blood, but if more than this was needed another container could be easily attached to an adaptor on the needle.

27 Contrary to prevalent opinion as to the amount of blood that could be safely transfused (between 300-500 cc.), Duran carried out transfusions with up to 3,000cc. of blood in a single, exsanguinated patient.

28 Triage was the system whereby the incoming wounded were sorted into three classes: those needing immediate attention, those who could be 'patched up' and evacuated to base hospitals and those for whom nothing could be done except ease their pain until they died.

29 Reg Saxton, transcript of interview for the Imperial War Museum, accession no. 008735/09, pp. 33–39.

30 Hank Rubin, *Spain's Cause was Mine: A Memoir of an*

American Medic in the Spanish Civil War, (Southern Illinois University Press, 1997), pp. 115-116.

31 Lillian Urmston, 'An English Nurse in Spain: Haemorrhage and Shock', *Nursing Mirror*, 10 June 1939, p. 368. At the end of the war, Duran was forced to flee into exile. British doctor Janet Vaughan facilitated Duran's invitation to Britain. She had been a medical volunteer in Spain where she became familiar with Duran's work. She was convinced that his knowledge and experience would be invaluable in the creation of a similar blood transfusion system in London, given the imminence of another world war. With Duran's help, she conceived a wartime blood supply system for use throughout the British Army and for civilian care.

32 This was Dr Vives i Nubiola, who was with Broggi's équipe for a short period.

33 Lillian does not say whether this was in one of the city's hospitals or at the Barcelona Blood Transfusion Service led by Dr Frederic Duran Jordà.

34 The apparatus devised by Duran for transfusing preserved blood in indirect transfusions could be used by any well-trained medical assistant.

35 Winifred Bates, 'Spanish Medical Aid Bulletin, March 1938', WDL 292/946/42/11.

Notes to Chapter Six

1 Monica Milward, 'Journey to Spain', July 1938, Alba Archives, Martin Coll, Box Z f.22, p.24.

2 Monica Milward, 'Some Notes on Spain', April 1970, Alba Archives, Martin Coll, Box Z f.23. p. 2.

3 Urmston, Tameside.

4 Bill Alexander, *British Volunteers for Liberty: Spain 1936-1939,* (London: Lawrence & Wishart Ltd, 1982), p.41.

5 Winifred Bates, 'Summary and Critical Survey of my work in Spain since the outbreak of the war': Barcelona, September 1938. Moscow Archives, Opis 6, F 88, p. 1.

6 Bates, 'Summary and Critical Survey', Moscow Archives, Opis 6, F 88 pp. 11-12.

7 Leah Manning, 'Report on Personnel in Spain', September 1938, WDL MSS 946/539.

8 Interview reel 2.

9 Bates, 'Summary and Critical Survey', Moscow Archives, Opis 6, F 88 p. 3.

10 Richard Baxell, 2007, p. 22.

11 Winifred Bates, 'Summary and Critical Survey', p. 4.

12 *Ibid*, p. 5.

13 Molly Murphy, *Molly Murphy: Suffragette and Socialist.* Institute of Social Research, University of Salford, Salford, 1998, p. 87.

14 Molly Murphy, letter from unnamed location in Spain to 'Dearest Bill & Gordon', dated 13 April 1937. British Online Archives. Debate and Division on the British Left, 1917-1964: URL:https://microform.digital/boa/collections/95/debate-and-division-on-the-british-left-1917-1964/key-data.

15 Richard Rees, A Theory of My Time: An Essay in Didactic Reminiscence. (London: Secker & Warburg, 1963), p. 95.

16 Rees, p. 104.

17 Rees, pp. 105-106.

18 Paul Preston, *Doves of War*, (London: HarperCollins, 2002), pp. 161-162.

19 Winifred Bates, 'Summary and Critical Survey'. Moscow Archives, Opis 6, F 88

20 Gerald Shirlaw, Testimonial for Lillian Urmston, 30 January 1940.

21 SMAC George Jeger (Organising Secretary) 12 April 1939

22 Evert Ruivenkamp, *Een Hollandse jongen aan de Ebro— Dagboek van een Spanjestrijder*, (Uitgeverij Jurgen Maas, 2022), p. 71.

23 *Ibid*, p. 74.

24 Lillian Urmston, 'An English Nurse in Spain: Travelling in Convoy', *Nursing Mirror*, 27 May 1939, p. 293.

25 Urmston, Tameside.

26 Urmston, Tameside.

27 Urmston, Tameside.

28 Urmston, Tameside.

29 During the Civil War, Hemingway wrote 31 dispatches from Spain, for the North American Newspaper Alliance (NANA). He also helped to produce a pro-Republican film, *The Spanish Earth,* and later used his experience in Spain to write his most famous novel, *For Whom the Bell Tolls.*

30 Urmston, Tameside.

31 Urmston, Tameside.

32 Latvian, Len Crome, studied medicine in Edinburgh. He went out to Spain initially with the Scottish Ambulance Unit but defected to the SMAC after disagreements with the Unit's administrator. As well as his medical expertise, Crome's brilliant organisational skills and ability to improvise led him to become Chief Medical Officer of the XV Army Corps.

Notes to Chapter Seven

1 Lillian Urmston, 'An English Nurse in Spain: Wounds', *Nursing Mirror*, 3 June 1939, p. 336.

2 P. Larraz and C. Ibarrola, 'Los pies de Teruel: Asistencia y tratamiento de las heridas por congelación en los hospitales navarros durante la guerra civil'. Extract published on the Internet; date unknown: http://www.requetes.com/sanidad. html.

3 Howard Keith Andrews was known affectionally as `Andy'. He used his Royal Army Medical Corps training to serve with the SMAC in frontline hospitals in Spain for over two years. He worked alongside Lillian with the surgeons Moisès Broggi, Alex Tudor-Hart and Doug Jolly. Lillian affirms that 'Andy' was in love with her American nursing colleague, Esther Silverstein.

4 In Jim Fyrth and Sally Alexander, *Women's Voices from the Spanish Civil War*, (London: Lawrence and Wishart, 1991), p. 75

5 Report by Winifred Bates, 'With the British and American Medical Aid at

Teruel', January 1938, Spanish Information Service. FMP, TL Series I, Box 2, Folder 23.

6 Urmston, Tameside.

7 Urmston, Tameside.

8 In Jim Fyrth and Sally Alexander, 1991, p. 76.

9 Winifred Bates, 'With the British and American Medical Aid at Teruel', January 1938, Spanish Information Service. (Fredericka Martin Papers, Tamiment Library, University of New York (FMP, TL), Series I, Box 2, Folder 23.

10 Emma Goldman, letter to the Manchester Guardian, 28 October 1936. Emma Goldman was born in Russia, of Jewish parents. She became an anarchist and was involved in trade union movements and in women's suffrage. She was 67 years old when she visited Spain upon the outbreak of civil war in 1936. There she met leading figures in the National Confederation of Labor and the Iberian Anarchist Federation (CNT–FAI) who invited her to direct their English propaganda campaign, from London. She was a tireless campaigner and wrote hundreds of letters to the media and publishers in the English-speaking world.

11 Spanish Medical Aid Bulletin for February 1939. WDL 292/946/42/4.

12 Urmston, Tameside.

13 Urmston, Tameside.

14 In Rémi Skoutelsky, *Novedad en el Frente. Las Brigadas Internacionales en la Guerra Civil,* (Madrid: Ediciones Temas de Hoy, S.A.), 2006, p. 151.

15 The exact extent of the problem will likely never be known, but see Paul Preston, *The Spanish Holocaust,* (London: HarperCollins Publishers Ltd), 2008.

16 Urmston, Tameside.

17 Winifred Bates, Spanish Medical Aid Committee Bulletin,

March 1938. WDL 292/946/42/11.

18 Spanish Medical Aid Committee Bulletin, May 1938. WDL 292/946/18b/28.

19 Urmston, Tameside.

20 *Ibid.*

21 The school was the CEIP Montsant, Avinguda de la Verge de Monserrat, Nº 2.

22 This was Catalan surgeon, Francisco Olsina Boher.

23 Reports received from Mrs Leah Manning and circulated to the committee in accordance with resolution 10th August 1938. Report No 1., 26th July 1938. WDL 292/946/42/16.

24 *Ibid.*

Notes to Chapter Eight

1 The Anschluss was the annexation of the Federal State of Austria into the German Reich on 13 March 1938.

2 Antony Beevor, *The Battle for Spain. The Spanish Civil War, 1936-1939*, (London: Penguin Books, 2006), pp. 349-350. Francoist prisoners would also be used to bolster numbers.

3 For a more detailed account of medical provisions for the battle of the Ebro, see Carles Hervás Puyal, 'The organisation of combat casualty care in the Republican Army', in Josep Sánchez Cervelló and Pere Clua Micola (eds), *The battle of the Ebro: A river of blood.* (Special 80th Anniversary Edition, Consorsi Memorial dels Espais de la Batalla de l'Ebre (COMEBE), 2018), pp. 117-126; Josep Munté-Mateu, 2021, pp. 159-168. For detailed explanation of the functioning of the 'three-points-forward

system', see D. W. Jolly, 1941.

4 Leah Manning, Report No 1. 26th July 1938. WDL 292/946/42/16.

The cave hospital has been the subject of more detailed study. See, for example, Angela Jackson, *Beyond the Battlefield: Testimony, Memory and Remembrance of a Cave Hospital in the Spanish Civil War*, (Warren & Pell Publishing, 2005). See also the memoirs of Nan Green, *A Chronicle of Small Beer*, (Nottingham: Trent Editions, Nottingham Trent University, 2005).

5 D. W. Jolly, 1941, p. 233.

6 Angela Jackson, 2005, p. 38.

7 Leah Manning, Report No 1. 26th July 1938. 10th AUGUST 1938. WDL 292/946/42/16.

8 *Ibid.*

9 Urmston, Tameside.

10 Winifred Bates, 'A woman's work in wartime', Marx Memorial Library, IBMT, Box 29/D/7.

11 Urmston, Tameside.

12 Lillian Urmston, SMAC Bulletin, October 1938. In Jim Fyrth and Sally Alexander, *Women's Voices from the Spanish Civil War*. (London: Lawrence and Wishart, 1991), p. 102.

13 Jolly 1941, p. 234.

14 Dr Gras documented all the injured cases he treated, from initial diagnosis to the outcome of intervention. From several handwritten notebooks preserved by his family, we learn that, between 25 and 29 July 1938, in the Santa Lucia cave hospital,

the surgeon attended to 25 wounded people, nine of whom died. He continued to record the cases treated in Mas de Santa Magdalena.

15 Josep Munté-Mateu, L'hospital del Mas de Santa Magdalena (Mora d'Ebre). *Miscel·lània del CERE* 31 (2021), pp. 159-168.

16 Fyrth & Alexander, 1991, p. 102.

17 *Ibid.*

18 Urmston, Tameside.

19 Fyrth & Alexander, 1991, p. 103.

20 Urmston, Tameside.

21 Lillian Urmston, 'An English Nurse in Spain: Travelling in Convoy', *Nursing Mirror*, 27 May 1939, p. 293.

22 Lillian Urmston, 'An English Nurse in Spain: Hospital in a Train Tunnel', *Nursing Mirror*, 17 June 1939, p. 403.

23 Lillian Urmston, 'An English Nurse in Spain: Hospital in a Train Tunnel', *Nursing Mirror*, 17 June 1939, p. 403.

24 Urmston, Tameside.

Notes to Chapter Nine

1 Urmston, Tameside.

2 Lillian Urmston, *Reporter*, 7 November 1938.

3 *Ibid.*

4 Lillian Urmston in the *Reporter*, 11 November 1938.

5 Urmston, Tameside

6 Beevor, 2006, p. 358.

7 Beevor 2006, p. 356.

8 Thomas, 2003, p. 832.

9 This lack of resources was exacerbated by the massive influx of refugees to Catalonia from other occupied areas.

10 Lillian Urmston, 'A nurse appeals for Spain', the *Reporter*, 17 December 1938.

11 Spanish Medical Aid Bulletin for February 1939. WDL 292/946/42/4.

12 Urmston, Tameside.

13 The International Brigades had been withdrawn and the remaining international volunteers were integrated in the Spanish Army units.

14 Beevor, 2006, pp. 375-376.

15 Alted, 2005, pp. 42-43.

16 Tuban, Grégory. *Camps d'étrangers: le contrôle des réfugiés venus d'Espagne (1939-1944)*, (París: Nouveau Monde Éditions, 2018), p. 33.

17 The origins of the Religious Society of Friends (or Quakers) can be traced to 17th century Britain. Precursors of the abolitionism of slavery, the Quakers are renowned for their pacifist beliefs and their commitment to humanitarian aid.

18 Friends' Service Council, 'Quaker Service in Spain, 1936-1940'. Friends' House Library, London: FSC/R/SP/5. See also the report of American Quakers: 'Annual Report—1939'.

Philadelphia: American Friends Service Committee, 1940, pp. 20-24.

19 Urmston, Tameside.

20 Paul Preston, 2002, p. 374.

21 Urmston, Tameside.

22 Rosita Davson, 'Report on the situation following the fascist offensive in Catalonia', Spanish Medical Aid Committee, 15 February 1939. WDL 292/946/43/33.

23 Letter from Edith Pye to Hilda Clark, 29 January 1939. In the papers of Hilda Clark, Friends House Library, (TEMP MSS 301, ASF).

24 Special correspondent, 'France Opens Frontier to Civilian Refugees', *Daily Telegraph*, 28 January 1939.

25 Preston 2002, p. 180.

26 Spanish Medical Aid Committee, 'Refugee Camps.' Bulletin March 1939. London: Marx Memorial

Library, box 29/B/14.

27 In Fyrth & Alexander, 1991, p. 333.

28 Vicente Fillol, *Los Perdedores: Memorias de un exiliado español*, (Madrid: Ediciones 'Gaceta Ilustrada', 1973), p. 8.

29 Urmston, Tameside.

30 On punishments and disciplinary camps, see Luiza Iordache Cârstea, 'Españoles tras las alambradas. Republicanos en los campos franceses, nazis y soviéticos (1939-1956)'. *Hispania Nova*, 1, 2019, pp. 27-28.

31 Tuban, 2018, p. 59. The declarations of Sarraut appeared in

La Dépêche, 2 February 1939.

32 Alted, 1997, p. 232.

33 Letter from Audrey Russell to the Friends' Service Council, 9 March 1939, Friends' House Library, London, FSC/R/SP/3/4.

34 Nancy Cunard, *Manchester Guardian*, 17 February 1919.

35 Wilson, Francesca, *In the Margins of Chaos. Recollections of Relief Work in and between Three Wars,* (London: John Murray, 1944), p. 220.

36 Vilanova i Vila-Abadal, Francesc, 'En el exilio: de los campos franceses al umbral de la deportación'. In Molinero, Carme, Sala, Margarita and Sobrequés, Jaume (eds.). *Una inmensa prisión. Los campos de concentración y las prisiones durante la guerra civil y el franquismo.* (Barcelona: Crítica, 2003), pp. 85-87.

37 Iordache, 2019, p. 28.

38 Urmston, Tameside.

39 Rosita Davson, 'Report on the situation following the fascist offensive in Catalonia', Spanish Medical Aid Committee, 15 February 1939. WDL 292/946/43/33.

40 Urmston, Tameside.

41 Urmston, Tameside.

Notes to Chapter Ten

1 Marks and Spencer had heard of Lillian, and they paid her to lecture. Urmston, Tameside.

2 Anonymous, 'Spanish Relief', *The Reporter*, 1 February 1939.

3 Anonymous, 'Spanish Relief Meeting at Petts Wood', *Bromley & West Kent Mercury*, Friday 17 March 139.

4 *Bromley & West Kent Mercury*, 31 March 1939.

5 For example, the *Tamworth Herald* (Saturday 24 June 1939), reported Lillian's talk on how to heat a ward or shock room with alcohol.

6 Anonymous, 'Bolingbroke Combined Action Station. Armistice Night Concert', *South Western Star*, Friday 17 November 1939.

7 Urmston, Tameside.

8 Gerald Shirlaw, Public Health Department. Letter of reference dated 8 February 1940.

9 Lillian Urmston, 'Back from France: T. A. N. S. Sister's Experience, *Nursing Mirror* 1 June 1940, p. 215.

10 Nurses want to go back to France, but told to stay in England, *Evening Standard*, 30 May 1940.

11 The railway line was built along the Khwae Noi (Kwai) River valley to support the Japanese armed forces during the Burma Campaign. Originally called the Thailand-Burma or Siam-Burma Railway, it earned the nickname 'Death Railway' because more than 12,000 Allied prisoners of war (POWs) and tens of thousands of forced labourers perished during its construction between 1942 and 1943.

12 Urmston, Tameside.

13 Max Collin, letter to John Buckoke dated 26 December 1990. In papers of Lillian Urmston, Museum of Military Medicine, Aldershot.

Notes to Appendix

1 In papers of Lillian Urmston, Museum of Military Medicine, Aldershot.

Select Index

(QUAIMNS) 22
Quemada, Dr 91, 106
Quinta del Biberón 102

Rees, Sir Richard 82-83
Relief Committee for Victims of Fascism 26
Republican Medical Service 39-43, 70, 77
Retirada (la) 117-132
Roquès, Pierre 42
Ruiz i Corto, Dr 110
Russell, Dr Audrey 129
Rutter, Dorothy 63, 92, 98
Ruivenkamp, Evert 85

Sabinosa 104, 123
Santa Lucía cave hospital 103, 115
Santa Magdalena see Mas de Santa Magdalena
Sarraut, Albert 129
Save the Children Fund 26
Saxton, Dr Reginald (Reg) 38, 61, 75-78, 91, 93, 99, 104-105
Servicio Sanitario de la República 39, 42
Servicio Sanitario Internacional (SSI) 42
Shirlaw, Dr Gerald see Jerry Steele
Sierra de Cavalls 110, 120
Sierra de la Vall de la Torre 120
Sierra de Pandols 120, 121
Silverstein, Esther 60, 92
Silverthorne, Thora 52
Sinclair-Loutit, Kenneth 59
Slater, Mary 132
SMAC – see Spanish Medical Aid Committee
Smythe, Jim 91
Smythe, Rosaleen 81, 90, 99
Socialists 24-25, 28, 38
Society of Friends – see Quakers

MEMORIES OF SPAIN SERIES AVAILABLE FROM THE CLAPTON PRESS

Perfidious Albion: Britain and the Spanish Civil War – Paul Preston

Forged in Spain – Richard Baxell

Never More Alive: Inside the Spanish Republic – Kate Mangan

The Good Comrade: Memoirs of an International Brigader – Jan Kurzke

In Place of Splendour – Constancia de la Mora

Firing a Shot for Freedom – Frida Stewart & Angela Jackson

The Fighter Fell in Love: A Spanish Civil War Memoir – James R Jump

The Last Mile to Huesca – Judith Keene and Agnes Hodgson

Struggle for the Spanish Soul – Arturo & Ilsa Barea

Hotel in Spain – Nancy Johnstone

Hotel in Flight – Nancy Johnstone

Sombreros are Becoming – Nancy Johnstone

Behind the Spanish Barricades – John Langdon Davies

Single to Spain & Escape from Disaster – Keith Scott Watson

Spanish Portrait – Elizabeth Lake

British Women in the Spanish Civil War – Angela Jackson

Boadilla – Esmond Romilly

My House in Málaga – Sir Peter Chalmers Mitchell

The Tilting Planet – David Marshall

Hampshire Heroes: Volunteers in the Spanish Civil War – Alan Lloyd

Remembering Spain: Essays, Memoirs and Poems on the International Brigades and the Spanish Civil War – edited by Joshua Newmark/IBMT

www.theclaptonpress.com